Living with Jan Hus

LIVING WITH JAN HUS

A *Modern* Journey Across a *Medieval* Landscape

THOMAS A. FUDGE

CCS

Center for Christian Studies
Portland, Oregon

2015

Published in 2015 by the Center for Christian Studies,
Portland, Oregon 97202

21 20 19 18 17 16 15   1 2 3 4 5 6 7

ISBN 13: 978 1-57896-281-5 (hardcover)
ISBN 10: 1-57896-281-1

Library of Congress Cataloguing-in-Publication Data
Fudge, Thomas A.
     Living with Jan Hus: A Modern Journey Across a
     Medieval Landscape/Thomas A. Fudge
     pages cm
     Includes bibliographical references (pages) and index.
     ISBN 13: 978 1-57896-281-5 (hardcover)
     ISBN 10: 1-57896-275-7

     1. Jan Hus, c.1372-1415. 2. Thomas A. Fudge. 3. Church
     history. 4. Biography and autobiography. 5. Theology,
     Doctrinal, controversies. 6. Church history-Europe-15th
     century. Title.

For Vern Yadon

colleague, friend, and intellectual companion
on the journey of life

Jan Hus, Old Town Square, Prague

Contents

Abbreviations

AAR	American Academy of Religion
BRRP	The Bohemian Reformation and Religious Practice
CBC	Conquerors Bible College
CCS	Center for Christian Studies
Documenta	František Palacký, ed., *Documenta Mag. Joannis Hus vitam, doctrinam, causam in constantiensi concilio actam et controversias de religione in Bohemia annis 1403-1418 motas illustrantia*
FRB	Fontes rerum bohemicarum
Hardt	Hermann von der Hardt, ed., *Magnum oecumenicum constantiense concilium*, 7 vols
MIHO	Magistri Iohannis Hus Opera Omnia
PDX	Portland, Oregon
SBL	Society of Biblical Literature
UNE	University of New England
WPC	Warner Pacific College

Illustrations

Acknowledgements and Foreword

A discredited legend had Jan Hus affirming at the pyre, and punning on his own name (the word "hus" in Czech means goose), that the Council of Constance would indeed roast a lean goose but in a hundred years hence a swan would sing and nothing would prevent that song.[1] The 600th anniversary of the death of Jan Hus has generated considerable and renewed attention on those events which culminated in Hus' death in 1415. The goose was cooked and some of Hus' detractors, the Franciscan preacher and inquisitor Giovanni Capistrano (1386-1456), for example, declared "the fat goose had been fried at Constance."[2] Early enthusiasm at the elimination of a perceived dangerous heretic soon turned to frustration. The Council inadvertently succeeded in creating a martyr whose steely resilience must have both shocked and dismayed late medieval Latin Christendom. More than a century later, following the unparalleled success of the Hussites in repelling five imperial crusades, a reformed ethos settling deeply into the religious fabric of Bohemia, the establishment of the popular sainthood of Hus and his inclusion in the liturgical practices of some

---

[1] The legend has been studied in Adolf Hauffen, "Husz eine Gans - Luther ein Schwan" *Prager Deutschen Studien* 9 (1908), pp. 1-28 and briefly summarized in Thomas A. Fudge, *Jan Hus: Religious Reform and Social Revolution in Bohemia* (London: I.B. Tauris, 2010), pp. 196-7.

[2] This appears in Giovanni Capistrano, *Epistola responsiva ad praefatam epistolam Johannis Borotini*, edited in František Wallouch, *Žiwotopis swatého Jana Kapistrána* (Brno: W Komissi u Ritsche a Grosse, 1858), p. 840.

Hussite communities, the invitation for Hussites to appear before an ecumenical council as equals with all of the sage men of Christendom, and the legal recognition of an alternative Christian Church in Bohemia, Martin Luther saw himself as the swan prophesied by Jan Hus and later sixteenth-century biographers of Luther appealed to the supposed prophesy as providing clear evidence of Luther's divine appointment and, by extension, validation of the Protestant Reformations.[3] Six centuries later, numerous manifestations of the swan continue to sing about the goose slain so long ago.

Jan Hus at 600 has provided opportunity to reflect on thirty years of research and to speak to audiences around the world about various aspects of Hus' life and legacy. This has been an enriching experience. Apart from an historiographical essay currently in progress, the bulk of my work on Hus

---

[3] There are several studies which illuminate the religious history of Bohemia after Hus. Howard Kaminsky, *A History of the Hussite Revolution* (Berkeley: University of California Press, 1967), Frederick G. Heymann, *John Žižka and the Hussite Revolution* (New York: Russell & Russell, 1969), Heymann, *George of Bohemia: King of Heretics* (Princeton: Princeton University Press, 1965), Otakar Odložilík, *The Hussite King: Bohemia in European Affairs, 1440-1471* (New Brunswick, NJ: Rutgers University Press, 1965), František M. Bartoš, *The Hussite Revolution 1424-1437*, trans. J. Weir, ed., John M. Klassen (New York: Columbia University Press, 1986), Gerald Christianson, *Cesarini: The Conciliar Cardinal, The Basel Years, 1431-1438* (St. Ottilien: EOS Verlag, 1979), Zdeněk V. David, *Finding the Middle Way: The Utraquists' Liberal Challenge to Rome and Luther* (Washington and Baltimore: Woodrow Wilson Center Press and Johns Hopkins University Press, 2003), and Thomas A. Fudge, *The Crusade Against Heretics in Bohemia, 1418–1437: Sources and Documents for the Hussite Crusades* (Aldershot: Ashgate, 2002).

has already appeared in four books devoted to him. However, the kind invitation to lecture in Portland, sponsored by CCS (Center for Christian Studies), provided opportunity to explore another facet of my work on late medieval Czech history. It also made

Fig. 1: Speaking at CCS, September 2015

possible a return to where my work on Hus had begun so many years ago and to the place where three of my four books on Hus had been written. The three books devoted to a medieval heretic had been written in the same office in an old building in the metro area and had once been described publicly as mainly "an abandoned, burned-out warehouse." The description was both creative and amusingly inaccurate. Of the several Portland engagements in September as a short-term scholar in residence at Reedwood Friends Church and CCS, the heart of this publication was presented as a public lecture. The response to that presentation was so uniformly positive and encouraging that discussions around possible publication ensued almost immediately.

This is a rather different kind of publication. It explores the life and thought of Hus while at the same time it attempts to explain how I came to devote so much of my professional life to the study of a dead priest. The Portland lecture attempted to trace part of my intellectual journey. The narrative deliberately shifts regularly from my own life in the modern world to the medieval context in which Hus flourished and it makes frequent forays into the medieval landscape in which Hus lived and which has compelled my attention as an historian. The narrative was simultaneously written as an essay designed to be presented in abbreviated fashion and adapted as a lecture. I utilized close to 200 visual images in the lecture presentation. A representative sampling of those pictures are included in this book. Initially, it was thought that the lecture would be published as a pamphlet but it was later decided the longer version of the original essay should appear along with some of the illustrations. This caused the length of the publication to far exceed pamphlet size and resulted instead in a small book. There are three justifications. First, it is all too rare for scholars to articulate their preoccupation with a topic and explain their work in the context of their own lives and intellectual pilgrimage. It is regrettable that too often such factors are regarded as unimportant and considered best left as part of one's private life. Second, it is often but erroneously assumed that historians have no personal commitment to their topics. However, there are always many reasons why particular topics are chosen and why certain interpretive methods are applied to those subjects. Third, the text which follows is a contribution to the historiography of Jan Hus. In my recent attempts to delineate the main trajectory of English-language scholarship on Hus over the past century and a half, I have discovered a number of frustrating lacunae especially when it came to finding out personal detail about authors and in the quest to try and explain how and why they went to the bother of writing, in this case, about Hus.

I am grateful to the steering committee of the Center for Christian Studies (CCS) together with Reedwood Friends Church for inviting and bringing me to Portland and for making publication of this monograph possible. I arrived in Portland for the CCS lectures Monday evening, 21 September 2015, exactly thirty-four years to the date and day of my first arrival in Oregon. More than three decades earlier, Jerry Peden, wearing a white dickey, picked me up. This time around, it was April Purtell, minus the dickey. I am indebted to the anonymous peer-reviewers for useful and insightful comments on the manuscript and for enabling me to present a more coherent and readable narrative. The flaws which doubtlessly remain are my own responsibility. Irv Brendlinger, Dwight Kimberly, and Kara Newall were each especially helpful in facilitating these Portland lectures. I am grateful to Louis G. Foltz and Stephen E. Lahey for granting permission to include their original artwork in this book. In what has become almost a tradition itself, Trish Wright has performed a fabulous job in making this book appear professional. Her skill and expertise in these matters has once again been drawn upon both with every confidence and to considerable benefit. She has also undertaken an entire battery of "research assistant" tasks with efficiency and enthusiasm. April Purtell not only advised on but assumed the technical responsibility for the dust jacket.

Tim Cluley managed to assemble an extremely rare gathering of individuals who are featured in an even rarer photo opportunity which appears in Fig. 26. This was only made possible because Professor Franz Bibfeldt mistakenly arrived in the year 2015, from Grossenknetten, for the 2016 *World Congress of the Oneness-Trinitarian Working Party* which had been scheduled to convene (but in the following year) to try and achieve (or relieve) the paradox and clarify the confusion of the role the Donnelley Stool may have played in the historic creation of a merger formed from two existentially non-existent entities in 1945. When advised of his chronological error, Bibfeldt merely said "perhaps" and suggested his confused colleagues dance to all tunes played in the headquarters of the old "Year Zero" club, and recite favorite passages from every *Herald*. Examining the newly discovered "merger agreement" documents (written in German by Bibfeldt) it now seems quite evident that Brother Bibfeldt, who was inexplicably airbrushed out of all the extant 1945 photographs, stands behind the text, in front of the text and is, in fact, the Ur-text itself. Whether the merger articles were committed to print in 1944, 1945, or 1946 has yet to be determined. Dr. Bibfeldt believes both/or.

One of the very best things in life is friendship. The famous Roman orator Marcus Tullius Cicero said that true friendship cultivates respect for truth and friendship becomes its own reward. Meaningful friendship has two necessary ingredients: virtue and loyalty. Only those who are virtuous and loyal can have true friends for these qualities are what one must give to another in order to experience *Amicitia* (friendship).[4] Jan Hus acquired a great friend while he was in Constance. This was Lord Jan Chlum, a Bohemian knight who served as an imperial escort and the two men, a soldier and an imprisoned priest, forged an unlikely relationship.[5] A number of years ago, when I had to live through a long dark night of the soul, I had the very good fortune of having no fewer than three extraordinary "Ciceronian friends." These good friends were April Purtell (of Prune Hill fame), Karyn O'Reilly-Lovell, and Vern Yadon. This little book is dedicated to the latter with lasting gratitude.

Thomas A. Fudge
Moravian Theological Seminary
Bethlehem, PA
31 October 2015

---

[4] Cicero. *De senectute, De amicitia, De divinatione*, translated by William Armistead Falconer [Loeb Classical Library, vol. 154] (Cambridge, MA: Harvard University Press, 1923), viii. 26-27, xiv.51, viii.26-28, xi.37-38, xiii.14, xiv.48-50, xvii.18, xviii.65, xxvii.100, and xxvii.104.

[5] I have explored this relationship in a chapter-length study in my book *Jan Hus Between Time and Eternity: Reconsidering a Medieval Heretic* (Lanham, MD: Lexington Books, 2016), pp. 117-140.

Introduction

Fixed in the city wall of Heraklion, on Crete, is a tomb marker which reads: Δεν ελπίζω τίποτα. Δε φοβούμαι τίποτα. Είμαι λέφτερος. Roughly translated it says "I hope for nothing. I fear nothing. I am free." This monument marks the final resting place of the Greek writer and philosopher Nikos Kazantzakis (1883-1957). Jan Hus was burned alive on a hot Saturday morning in the summer of 1415. The Brüel Field used to be a wide open expanse outside the city walls of Constance. There is now a large boulder marking the spot in a quiet residential neighborhood. I have stood before the stone many times over many years. Like Kazantzakis, Jan Hus hopes for nothing. He fears nothing. He is free. I am not. As one who has studied Hus for three decades, I still hope, I still fear, and I am not free.

In northern Bohemia there is a hill which towers above the small villages. There is a splendid view of

Fig. 2: Ruins of Kalich Castle, 1991

the surrounding countryside from the top. Green and yellow fields seem to stretch to the horizon and there are villages here and there among the basalt rock promontories which for centuries have guarded these northern Czech lands like silent sentinels. In 1421, Hussite armies conquered the small wooden fortress which once stood on the hilltop, owned by the Knights of the Teutonic Order. It was rebuilt in stone and renamed "Kalich" (chalice) reflecting the main theological point of the Hussite faith. It came under the control of the military commander Jan Žižka. Hus had been dead half a dozen years at this point but the chalice at the top of this steep wooded hill gave silent witness, both then and now, to the enduring presence of a dead priest.

PART ONE

Jan Hus was a Bohemian priest executed 600 years ago following a five year legal ordeal wherein he was found guilty of heresy. The culmination of that trial occurred during the Council of Constance, which sat between 1414 and 1418, and which may be considered one of the greatest assemblies of the entire Middle Ages.

I encountered Jan Hus briefly as a boy, more seriously as a college student, and then in earnest as a young man seeking to find my way through the world of higher education with an eye on becoming an academic. As my Mother used to say, "there has been a lot of water under the bridge since then." Much of that water has been filled with reflections of images from another world, a medieval world, one long ago and very far away shrouded in the forgetfulness of things past. That world finds its roots in the fabled land of Bohemia, among Slavic peoples, and especially among those long-dead men and women some scholars have called Hussites. These Hussites took their name from this man Jan Hus.

Fig. 3: Burning of Hus, Ulrich Richental, *Chronicle of the Council of Constance*, Prague, National Library
MS XVI A 17, fol. 123v

Several decades have passed since those early discoveries. In this hectic year of the sexcentenary of Hus' death and the rigorous demands on my time and energy, I came to the awareness one day that I had, in some sense, been living with Jan Hus. That realization reminded me of the title of a memoir written by my friend and colleague Professor Jiří

Kejř in 2012 called *I Lived in the Middle Ages.*[6] In this book, Kejř looked back over ninety years of life and his career as an expert in medieval canon law wherein he too cultivated a keen interest in Jan Hus and these same Hussites. *Living with Jan Hus* has afforded me with the quite unusual opportunity to remember, recognize and reflect.

Within the professional academy there is a distinct awkwardness about a subjective and personal engagement with history and the suspicion that such approaches are unscholarly and thereby suspect and of little value and those who engage in this manner with the past are not proper scholars at all or if they are then such distractions are the purview of old men and women reminiscing on glory days. Norman Cantor caused a storm of controversy in 1991 when he suggested the Middle Ages were invented and went on to deal with twenty medievalists whom he argued created the current perception of medieval Europe.[7] From the fallout of *Inventing the Middle Ages*, Cantor felt compelled to write a second book titled *Inventing Norman Cantor.*[8] Does Hus need to be invented? He is the hero of a dozen faces: Communist, rebel, Roman Catholic, nationalist, symbol of freedom, Czech national hero, firm religious reformer, social revolutionary, Evangelical Christian, disciple of Wyclif, Protestant, heretic, or a saint. Hus is all of these things and more to different people and has

---

[6] Jiří Kejř, *Žil jsem ve středověku* (Prague: Academia, 2012).

[7] Norman F. Cantor, *Inventing the Middle Ages: The Lives, Works, and Ideas of the Great Medievalists of the Twentieth Century* (New York: William Morrow, 1991).

[8] Norman F. Cantor, *Inventing Norman Cantor: Confessions of a Medievalist* (Tempe: Arizona Center for Medieval and Renaissance Research, 2002).

been since the moment of his immolation. I have tried to be objective in my assessment of Hus. That in itself is a challenge of no mean proportion. A fifteenth-century hagiographical account of Hus, suggests that "the Lord God almighty, wanting to shed light upon the truth by being known again, introduced a faithful man by the name of Jan Hus, whom he put up as a burning candle in a gold chandelier, in order to shine a light for all those who are in the house and who wish to come to the knowledge of the faith."[9] One must be wary of constructing an act of overt homage and inventing a portrait in our own image, rather than discovering the historical figure. It is true that monuments are often built to honor figures after their deaths from the stones hurled at them while they were alive. There is also a dangerous myopia associated with focusing on the life of an individual which can obscure the historical context in which that person lived.

Jan Hus was born in Husinec, a small village of no importance in southern Bohemia. The streets are quiet, the buildings plain, ordinary, and one can stand there for some time and hear nothing but birds chirping, and the gentle breeze rustling through the

---

[9] *"Život, to jest šlechetné obcování ctného svatého kněze, Mistra Jana Husi, kazatele českého, od kněze Jiříka Heremity, věrného kazatele českého, sepsaný a nyní v nově vytištěný"* [The life and holy conduct of the honorable and holy priest Master Jan Hus, Czech preacher, by the priest George the Hermit, faithful Czech preacher, written and now printed again]. The text was published in Jaroslav Goll, et al., eds., *Fontes rerum bohemicarum*, 8 vols (Prague: Nákladem nadání Františka Palackého, 1873-1932), vol. 8, pp. 377-83, at p. 377. Hereafter, FRB. For background on the text, see Thomas A. Fudge, *The Memory and Motivation of Jan Hus, Medieval Priest and Martyr* (Turnhout: Brepols, 2013), pp. 189-90.

branches of linden trees. The ruins of a fourteenth-century castle, destroyed in 1441, can still be seen situated on a rock above the Blanice River. There is little to indicate that perhaps the most famous Czech of all time was born here and played with other children six-and-a-half centuries ago. In speaking of Jan Hus, it is important to reveal aspects of the medieval man while simultaneously opening up a wider view of his place during the time he lived. There is also the danger of emotional identification which may cloud the scholar's objectivity and limit his or her perspective. All such potential challenges must be recognized, confronted, and overcome.

Whatever distance one is expected to maintain from a subject of inquiry there is no gainsaying that writers create an impression of themselves through choices of style and the content of their work in the same way that scholars may reveal something of themselves in the subjects they research. But what do we reveal? Until recently, I would never have considered doing a public lecture like this had I not unexpectedly encountered a book by the leading historian of Hussitica in a Prague bookshop wherein he evaluated his own work by engaging in what he described himself as an intentional delineation of the "findings, encounters and coincidences in the life of a medievalist."[10] A few days later I heard a lecture on 6 July 2015 in Prague wherein another scholar spoke openly and at length about his role in

---

[10] František Šmahel, *Nalézání, setkávání a míjení v životě jednoho medievisty* (Prague: Argo, 2009), especially pp. 443-65.

the European-wide reconsideration of the post-Marxist Hus in the 1990s.[11]

Another motivation comes from the strange anonymity of scholars in the past who lived and died on dates difficult to determine, whose lives went largely unrecorded and whose interest in certain topics remain essentially unknown. Beyond these challenges, there are few clues to inform our understanding of who these scholars and writers really were.[12] Sometimes the gaps in sources from the nineteenth and early twentieth centuries are just as severe as those which routinely complicate medieval sources. These biographical lacunae are a loss to historiography for the simple reason that those who write histories also shape history. With that caveat, this small book is offered as a modest contribution to the historiography of Jan Hus.

Historians simply cannot avoid living with their characters or interacting with their subjects. That association may be fleeting like the actor who throws off the costume when the play is done or promptly forgets his or her lines once filming has concluded. Other, scholarly, encounters or work may assume more permanent dimensions. Hus left behind no account of his life, no autobiography, and no memoir. He did not emulate St. Augustine's

---

[11] Jan Blahoslav Lášek at an event which was part of the 600th anniversary of Hus. The lecture convened in the Church of St. Nicholas in the Old Town. Lášek edited the important 1993 Bayreuth symposium papers as *Jan Hus mezi epochami, národy a konfesemi* (Prague: Česká křesťanská akademie: Husitská teologická fakulta Univerzity Karlovy, 1995).

[12] While researching English-language historiography I have encountered numerous gaps wherein little to nothing could be discovered about obscure men like James Hamilton Wylie and Eustace J. Kitts for example.

Confessions, replicate Peter Abelard's *Story of My Misfortunes*, or prefigure Karl Barth's book *How My Mind Has Changed*. The quest of the historical Hus can be as frustratingly elusive as the quest of the historical Jesus as once convincingly argued by Albert Schweitzer. How does one come to form a thirty-year commitment to evaluating the life, ideas, and legacy of Jan Hus? How and why does one end up living with Jan Hus? This lecture, then, is chiefly about a modern encounter with a medieval figure, combining the historical biography of Hus with the intellectual autobiography of one who has attempted to understand Hussite history. This lecture is a brief chronicle of my own journey from naïve teenage curiosity about Jan Hus to a mid-life position where I have been surprised to find myself characterized in terms of an internationally "renowned expert" and "authority" about a dead priest who lived long ago and far away in a place we call the Middle Ages.

Fig. 4: Rábi Castle, 14th century, SW Czech Republic

Throughout Bohemia, there are silent ruins of the castles and fortresses which once belonged to men and women prepared to die for the faith of Jan Hus. Down one lonely country road, and across a green wind-swept field, and almost completely hidden by a small wood, lies the remains of Sión Castle. Here in 1437, the last Hussite warrior, Jan Roháč of Dubá, and a small hardy band of men unwilling to surrender, were finally defeated and taken away to the gallows. Sión Castle sits on the brow of a cliff. Approaching from the field there is no indication that just beyond the ring of trees and beyond the worn stone ruins, the landscape changes radically. There is a stream at the bottom of the cliff and a trail that winds its way through the wood. Were it not for a posted sign in Czech, no one today would know that the last fight of the old Hussite warriors took place above the cliff facing the open expanse of the green wind-swept field.

"In the year of the Lord 1403 there arose a notable dissension ..."[13] This pithy comment in a fifteenth-century chronicle refers to the controversy over John Wyclif at Charles University in Prague. We cannot know if Hus was ever asked directly why he was attracted to John Wyclif. More times than I can recall over the course of my career, I have been asked why I am interested in Jan Hus and Hussite history. On a very regular basis I am asked if I am of Czech descent. It is assumed this must be the root cause of my interest in Hussite history. To the best of my slight knowledge, there are no Slavic elements in my ancestry. So far as I can tell, my paternal Fudges and maternal Wallaces are both Scottish, several generations deep. So far as we know, Hus' parents were Czech but their names

---

[13] Noted in the Chronicle of the University of Prague, in FRB, vol. 5, p. 569.

have long disappeared into the mists of the past.
Instead of a cultural impulse, I believe my attraction
to Hus came via my religious upbringing, albeit in a
rather circuitous fashion. Jan Hus' own career as a
churchman was probably stimulated by the piety of
his mother. I grew up in a household of "heresy."
My boyhood years were filled with religion, church,

Fig. 5: With my brother David, Harvey Lake,
New Brunswick, 1973

rules, regulations, expectations, pastoral pressure,
doctrinal demands, and theological peculiarities.
My earliest memories of the world were fashioned
on a church pew. At home, we observed the daily
ritual of family devotions, as it was called, wherein
my parents and two siblings read scripture aloud
before also praying aloud. We were never permitted
to depart for school before Mother read a passage of
scripture aloud to us and prayed for us. Hus tells us

that his mother taught him to pray and encouraged him to become a priest.[14] And there were books. I can still recall my father's thick copy of Matthew Henry's commentary on the entire Bible, its green and pink cover, published in 1961 spanning almost 2,000 pages (I marveled at its sheer size), together with Merrill C. Tenney's smaller orange-colored 1963 *Pictorial Bible Dictionary*, both volumes published by the Christian evangelical Zondervan press. While Hus does mention his mother in his writings, he makes no reference to his father. It would be improper to conclude his father exerted no influence on the young Hus. The significance of Hus' silence is impossible to assess but it may be compared to the religious influence his mother had

Fig. 6: With my father in Boston, 1987

on him.[15] I have vivid recollections of following my father into one used bookshop after another in New England and I too soon became an inveterate book

---

[14] Matthew Spinka, *John Hus: A Biography* (Princeton: Princeton University Press, 1968), p. 22.

[15] *Menší výklad na páteř*, in *Magistri Iohannis Hus Opera omnia*, 27 vols (Prague: Academia, and Turnhout: Brepols, 1959-), vol. 1, p. 392. Hereafter MIHO.

collector, addicted to dusty shelves and the tomes of learning from the past.

I mentioned that I was raised in a household of heresy. That heresy was double-layered. First, there was the "movement" my parents had come into around 1964. It was called a "movement" and my father routinely referred to the fact that he and Mother "came in" to the "movement." The term denomination was never used with reference to the fellowship of churches. Instead, we were part of the "organization." The "organization" stood solidly behind the "message" and it was the "message" which was the most important thing in the entire world. That was impressed upon me rather firmly as a small boy. My parents had been Anglican and they migrated to the "organization" by way of the Canadian United Baptist Church. All said, by 1964 my father had presented himself for baptism for the third time (Anglican christening as an infant, triune immersion in the Baptist church as an adult, and immersion once more in the name of Jesus as a Oneness Pentecostal). From then on, he and Mother were truly in the "movement" and were part of the "organization" and were now firm believers in the "message," or so I assumed. I was far too young to remember any of this but I was nurtured by the "organization," truly believed the "message" (in my naïve youthful way), and was embraced by a religious orientation that was all-encompassing. At one stage as a teenager, I attended church twice on Sunday (with the evening service regularly lasting three hours), had choir practice on Monday evening and on Tuesday evening I routinely attended Bible study. Wednesday evening was outreach and I joined the faithful in knocking on doors and inviting local misfortunates to obey the "message," join the "organization," and come into the true "movement." Thursday evening was a youth service. Fridays were free but Saturday evening was a prayer service. In other words, I was fully indoctrinated into a version of the Christian faith and practice. This helps to partly explain my eventual interest in Church History. I discovered that Hus was just as religious and utterly committed to the "message" of the later medieval church. As a poor student, he spent his last few remaining coins to buy an indulgence after listening to a particularly powerful and persuasive sermon at Vyšehrad, on the south side of Prague.[16]

A generation later, some followers of Jan Hus founded the city of Tábor, situated about sixty miles directly south of Prague. We are fortunate to have a description from the fifteenth century.

> He [Jan Žižka] surrounded it with ramparts and ordered everyone to build their houses the same way they earlier had erected their tents. He gave the town the name of Tábor ... Though the town is protected by tall rocks, it is surrounded by walls and moats. The river Lužnice runs around the larger part of the town, a quite large and rapid stream runs around the remaining part. It aims straight towards Lužnice, but because rocks obstruct its way alongside the whole town, it is forced to turn to the right and it empties into the larger river at the end of town. The neck (both streams form a peninsula) is not more than thirty feet wide. There is an artificial ditch and triple wall so thick that no machine of siege can break through. There are many towers on the walls and fortifications (bastions) at suitable places, which the Táborites, masters in conquering towns, invented themselves. This way Žižka was the first to build a refuge for all heretics and a castle; those who

---

[16] *Chronicon universitatis pragensis*, FRB, vol. 5, p. 568.

followed him improved the fortifications of the town, each of them as he was capable of doing it.[17]

One cannot stand in Tábor today and not be mindful of the Hussite heritage. Medieval tunnels run below the main square where an impressive

Fig. 7: Stone table at Tábor: with Jeanne Grant, Stephen Lahey, and Henry Gerlach, 2015

statue of Jan Žižka welcomes visitors to the historic town center. Two stone tables provide silent witness to the Táborite practice of communal sharing of all things as a requirement for joining the community. A late Gothic medieval structure, and former Town Hall, is now a museum dedicated to the history of the Hussite movement. This building dominates the west parameter of the square. Beyond this, through narrow medieval streets, one can reach the remains of the old walls and the fifteenth-century tower that

---

[17] Enea Sylvio, *Historia bohemica*, eds., Dana Martínková, Alena Hadrovová, and Jiří Matl (Prague: KLP, 1998), chapter 40, pp. 114-16.

once greeted travellers and visitors and signaled a tradition of defiance.

I noted earlier, that I was raised in a household of heresy. The "organization" tended to think that it alone had truth. Other Christians might be saved but

Fig. 8: St. Cyril defeats the heretic.
Church of St. Nicholas, Prague (Lesser Town)

this was by no means certain. The "message" was divine revelation. The road was narrow and few were able to find it. The broad road led straight to destruction and there were many poor, deceived and erring souls who wound up following that way. This included most Christians and all non-Christians. I never heard the name Jan Hus mentioned either in

church or in any of the literature provided by the
publishing house of the "organization." In fact,
there was very little at all about history or historical
awareness. Indeed, the solitary thing I recall clearly
was the often-spoken conviction that our church
was apostolic, that it represented an unbroken line
of continuity extending back to the day of Pentecost
and the early church as reflected in the biblical Acts
of the Apostles. The problem was, as I learned only
much later, it was extremely difficult to trace the
"message" throughout the history of the church, and
the "organization" had only come into existence in
1945. From a historical/theological perspective, the
"message" was heresy and the "organization" was
clearly heretical, when judged by the mainstream of
church history. Exclusive claims to truth, a strident
judgmental attitude towards doctrinal difference,
and the inability to defend the "message" biblically,
theologically or historically, meant that I was a real
junior heretic. However, this heritage also implied
that I was ever more inclined to take the heretics of
church history seriously. After all, they too had
been persecuted for the cause of righteousness by a
false church just as surely as the beleaguered
"organization" had been ridiculed by the apostate
contemporary church world while the "message"
was woefully and shamefully ignored. Still, I knew
virtually nothing about heresy and I did not possess
awareness that I was a little heretic and that most of
the people I knew were also heretics.

One more additional comment should be made
concerning the household of heresy. As it turned
out, my father was something of a heretic himself
within a heresy. He was not at all convinced that the
"organization" possessed all definite theological
truth and it was manifestly clear that he considered

those outside the "movement" also to be good
Christians, definitely saved, and just as eligible for
salvation as anyone within the "organization." He
even considered Catholics to be his brothers and
sisters and while he clearly rejected the doctrine of
the Trinity, he did not exclude Trinitarians from the
body of Christ. In short, my father was weak on the
"message." Much later, I heard that our pastor had
once remarked privately that it had to be borne in
mind that "Brother Fudge had been an Anglican for
many years." Ostensibly, this helped to explain his
suspect standing within the "organization" and on
critical matters like the "message."

I mentioned the books in my boyhood home
previously. Among the volumes which I perused
was a condensed version of a famous account of
Christian martyrs. This was John Foxe's *Acts and
Monuments* which had appeared in 1563 and was a
landmark Elizabethan work.[18] In its time, it was the
largest book ever to be conceived and published in
English with a text which ran to over two million
words. The title page of the *Acts and Monuments*
sets forth Foxe's intention of describing "the great
persecutions & horrible troubles, that have been

---

[18] Four editions of the *Acts and Monuments of these latter and
perilous days, touching matters of the church, wherein are
comprehended and described the great persecutions and
horrible troubles, that have been wrought and practised by the
Romish Prelates, specially in this Realm of England and
Scotland, from the year of our Lord a thousand, unto the time
now present* were published during Foxe's lifetime. These
publications appeared in 1563, 1570, 1576 and 1583. The four
editions are not simple reprints and often are quite different
presentations. A new online critical edition now supersedes all
previous printed editions. *The Unabridged Acts and
Monuments Online* or *TAMO* (HRI Online Publications,
Sheffield, 2011). Available from: http//www.johnfoxe.org

wrought and practiced by the Roman Prelates."
Chained copies of the book were ordered placed in
cathedrals and in homes of the chapter clergy by the
Privy Council in 1571. Francis Drake took a copy of
the book with him around the world in 1577. The
Acts and Monuments achieved a status close to that
of a second Bible.[19] One might even say "Foxe's
Acts and Monuments did not create a legend; it
commemorated a truth."[20] As a young boy, I knew
this weighty work by its shorthand title "Foxe's
Book of Martyrs." There is some chance, I saw the
name Jan Hus therein, but all I recall are stories
about faithful Christians persecuted by the wicked
Catholics. I knew I had to steer clear of such people,
cling fervently to the "message," adhere firmly to
the "organization," and never entertain doubts about
the truths inculcated by the fiery men of God who
regularly mounted the pulpit and assured us that we
were firmly ensconced on the straight and narrow
way which led irrevocably to salvation.

What I can clearly recall is obtaining a copy of
Roland H. Bainton's celebrated biography of Martin
Luther.[21] That was in 1976. I was fourteen years
old. I felt some attraction to Luther and the tale of
his life. In that book there are references to Jan Hus,
whose work Luther was aware of and Luther had
considerable praise for Hus. Still, Bainton's *Luther*
awakened my young mind to the world of sixteenth-
century Germany not to the shadowy land beyond
the Bohemian Forest. What was significant, though,

---

[19] Tessa Watt, *Cheap Print and Popular Piety, 1550-1640*
(Cambridge: Cambridge University Press, 1991), p. 90.
[20] Geoffrey Elton, *Reform and Reformation* (London: Edward
Arnold, 1977), p. 386.
[21] Roland H. Bainton, *Here I Stand: A Life of Martin Luther*
(Nashville: Abingdon, 1950).

was the fact that in 1976 as I was reading Bainton, my father received our pastor into our home and a theological discussion took place. The conversation revolved around the "message" as proclaimed by the "organization." At a particular juncture, being within earshot of the conversation and my mind being stimulated by the exchange, I reached a point where I was no longer reading Roland Bainton but eavesdropping on a clear disagreement. In short, my father was denying the essence of the "message" and nothing the pastor could say was sufficient to dislodge my father from his own convictions. It was at that point in my life when I realized I was the son of a bona fide heretic. That realization produced neither revulsion nor fear. Secretly, I felt a sense of pride. The irony, of course, was that I was holding in my teenage hands at that very moment a book about the single greatest heretic in the history of the church up to the sixteenth century. Perhaps from that moment on, I began to cultivate private doubts about the "message" myself and, following my father's example, began to question certain other unique features of the "organization." What is quite certain, is that Roland Bainton had prompted me to take Martin Luther seriously. I wrote a term paper on Luther for Mr. (Greg) Theobald's History class in Grade Ten, at Saint John High School, and every now and then dipped into *Here I Stand* and slowly but surely imbibed more of the ethos of Luther and the Reformation. It proved to be highly toxic to "the message" and eventually undermined my youthful and naïve certainty. The ex-monk Martin Luther and my own father had inadvertently conspired to set me upon a road of exploration and discovery.

Prachatice sits very close to Husinec. Here, the young Hus studied.[22] A later hagiographical account of Jan Hus' life asserts that from the time he was a child, Jan Hus was given to the Lord God by

Fig. 9: Prachatice, Czech Republic

his mother in the same manner as Hannah offered the future Samuel the prophet. Hus' mother led the child to school and carried a loaf of bread for the schoolmaster. Before she reached Prachatice, she knelt seven times and prayed for her son, and begged God to guide him to his honor and praise for the benefit of all the people.[23] Prachatice is a typical Czech town dominated by a large central square, red-roofed buildings, narrow, winding streets and passageways, all exuding a faint hint of its medieval past. The Gothic spires of the Church of St. James dominate the skyline. Jan Žižka and radical Hussites

---

[22] František M. Bartoš, "Hus jako student a profesor Karlovy university" *Acta universitatis carolinae – philosophica et historica* 2 (1958), pp. 9-10.
[23] "The Life of Jan Hus by George the Hermit," in FRB, vol. 8, p. 377.

burned down parts of Prachatice in the year 1420 and also demolished some of the walls.

At length, I departed from my boyhood home in Maritime Canada, went to the American west coast and came to Oregon. Luther was in the back of my mind, vaguely, while Jan Hus was barely a name I recognized. I was still under the influence of the "message" and more or less a faithful member of the "organization." Theology was not on my mind and church history remained almost as vague as ever. I took up what I imagined might evolve into a career in church music at the virtually unknown and singularly unimpressive Conquerors Bible College in Portland. As a young student, Jan Hus apparently

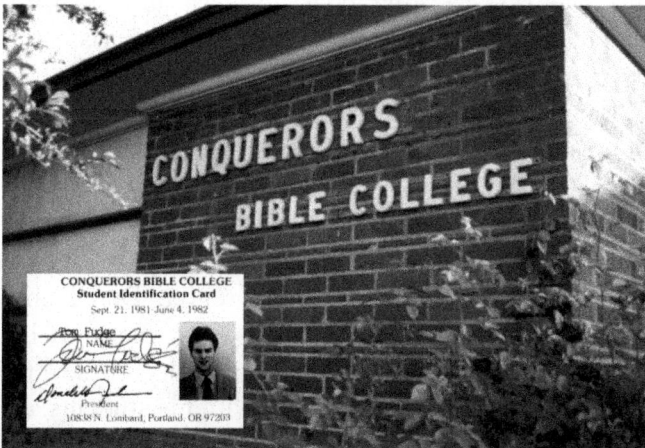

Fig. 10: CBC campus and student I.D. card

supported himself as a singer in one of the churches in Prachatice.[24] My career in music was short-lived. I completed two years as a music major but those youthful dreams were fading fast. I applied myself to my studies but I spent more time carousing into the wee hours, in the custom of college students,

---

[24] Spinka, *John Hus: A Biography*, p. 24.

than doing my music homework. I spent some time in the college library but hardly enough for anyone to accuse me of devotion to scholarship. We learn from Hus' own pen of his dalliances with mischief and participation in public scandals and what he describes as foolishness.[25]

At length, several events of personal world-shaking importance occurred in Portland. These led to another sort of conversion. The first was coming directly under the growing influence of the college president, Don Fisher. Fisher was all of forty-two years of age when we first shook hands during a social function held on 21 September 1981. This occurred on the old CBC campus following my first airplane ride, a long coast-to-coast junket, from Saint John, Canada to PDX. Fisher was charismatic, dynamic, an effective leader with a reputation for getting things done but also known for inspiring young people to achievements beyond their own small expectations. I would later number Fisher among the important influences and mentors in my life. His untimely demise at age fifty-six was a matter of considerable personal regret. Don Fisher formed meaningful relationships with many of his students. This is conducive to maturity on several levels. Jan Hus worked closely with his students. At least thirty-six of them were graduated under his tutelage.[26] In his promotion speeches, Hus displays humor and a level of familiarity with his charges. For example, on 22 January 1400, Václav Sušice graduated. Master Hus mentioned Václav's short stature, the type of clothes he wore and his physical

---

[25] *Výklad na Páteř*, in MIHO, vol. 1, p. 342.
[26] Bartoš, "Hus jako student a profesor Karlovy university," p. 17.

appearance, while warning the graduand to pursue the life of the mind and spirituality while avoiding the pleasures of the flesh. In the case of the student

Fig. 11: Don Fisher and C.H. Yadon, c.1978

Martin Kunšov, Jan Hus again commented on his physical appearance and noted that the "lazy and sleepy" Martin had needed six years to complete his studies. Nevertheless, the graduand was a young man of both honesty and virtue. In 1405, Zdislav of Zvířetice was promoted and Hus likewise remarked on his laziness, pointing out he often had to awaken Zdislav from his slumber.[27] Don Fisher always kept everyone awake in his classes. I cannot remember anyone who ever went to sleep on Fisher.

---

[27] Hus' speeches have been edited in Anežka Schmidtová, ed., *Iohannes Hus, Magister universitatis carolinae: Positiones, Recommendationes, Sermones* (Prague: Státní pedagogické nakladatelství, 1958), and the ones noted here appear on pp. 51-61.

I also came under the more subtle influence of one of my other professors, Charles Haskell (C.H.) Yadon (1908-1997). He was past seventy-four years of age when I met him. Within the "organization," he was a towering presence, respected, revered in some quarters, a real thinker, and a man who knew something about Hus though I do not recall him ever talking about Jan Hus in his lectures. He did mention Hus in a sermon once. His words seemed like a gentle rebuke to the arrogance and historical presumption within the "organization." He rather firmly admonished his hearers thus: "We...ought to inform ourselves a little more about church history. There have been some people on this earth that loved God before we ever showed up. And you read about John Hus. You read about the Waldensians and others... Martin Luther... History is full of this."[28] C.H. Yadon was an old cowboy who had come from Indian Territory in Oklahoma who lived in a bunkhouse from time to time, punched cattle in Nevada, and later took up residence in Rock Creek Canyon in southern Idaho with the notoriously heretical Yadon family. Fisher and Yadon met me at a vocational and spiritual crossroads and pointed me in another direction. I did not know this at the time, of course, but looking back now over the years, both were men who contributed to my future living with Jan Hus.

Behind the walls of medieval towns, men and women talked about Jan Hus, about his preaching, his challenge to the church, and perhaps what it meant for their lives. In these communities, which

---

[28] C.H. Yadon, "Fire That Will Never Go Out," sermon at the United Pentecostal Church Idaho District camp meeting, in McCall, Idaho, on 22 July 1982.

still remain as modern monuments to the medieval past, the turrets are now empty, vines grow on walls which no longer ward off intruders. The old stone

Fig. 12: Nymburk, Czech Republic, city walls

buildings are silent. The squares of these towns are often empty now and they are no longer places for people to congregate, to hear the news, to discuss their hopes and fears. Popular preachers no longer deliver homilies and the vineyards outside the walls are more a topic of conversation than theology.

Jan Hus does not speak of a specific conversion experience though he does refer to transitions in his own thought. For example, Hus desired a career in the priesthood in order to achieve a reasonable standard of living, be able to dress respectably, and to be held in the esteem of others.[29] He set aside his fondness for entertainment, games, playing chess, and taking part in activities he eventually deemed unprofitable.[30] Of further note, is that for a time he

---

[29] *O svatokupectví*, in MIHO, vol. 4, p. 228.

[30] See his letter to his former pupil Martin Volyně, which may be dated to early October 1414, in Václav Novotný, ed., *M. Jana Husi Korespondence a dokumenty* (Prague: Nákladem komise pro vydávání pramenů náboženského hnutí českého,

enjoyed the esteem of his priestly colleagues in Prague as well as the obvious favor of his ordinary, Archbishop Zbyněk. However, he soon found the innate boldness to speak out against abuses and the irregularities which he perceived as existing in the church. Once this began, he fell into disfavour and many clerics attacked him insisting that he was possessed by the Devil and had become a heretic.[31]

In 1977, a film about Jan Hus, sponsored by a Christian company, was released. That very short film was shown at CBC or at CBC events at least

Fig. 13: Hus monument, Old Town Square,
Prague, 1915, by Ladislav Šaloun

three times during my student tenure.[32] I remember it vividly. It is not a very good film. It is historically and theologically inaccurate in many respects but it

---

1920), pp. 204-205, and *Výklad na Páteř*, in MIHO, vol. 1, p. 342.

[31] František M. Bartoš, ed., *Listy Bratra Jana a Kronika velmi pěkná a Janu Žižkovi* (Prague: Blahoslav, 1949), p. 36.

[32] *Journal of Thomas A. Fudge, 1980-1985*, with entries for 3 December 1981, 30 January 1982, and 26 February 1983.

made a deep impression. The third time I viewed the film I had tears in my eyes as I contemplated the courage of conviction, the unswerving allegiance to principle, the robust unyielding fidelity to truth. The film starred Rod Colbin (1923-2007) as Jan Hus. To this day, I see the face of Rod Colbin whenever I think of Hus. Following this portrayal, I determined to find out more about this man and attempt to see how his life might inform mine.

The last thing about my experiences at CBC which were fundamental for my own development was my discovery that CBC itself had a growing reputation for being weak on the "message" and an institution generating grave suspicion within the "organization." Fisher and Yadon were the prime suspects. By mid-March 1983, CBC had closed its doors. C.H. Yadon was a kindly, grandfatherly heresiarch, but he was a heretic nonetheless, and his disciple Fisher, who had already been compared to Jan Hus, was a liability to the "movement" and even more dangerous than his mentor. Both men were extremely weak on the "message." Both would later leave the "organization." The college campus was bulldozed in 1985.[33] I left CBC with Jan Hus in my mind and with a growing determination to discover truth. I could not realize that intellectual journey would exact a high cost and require a lifetime. Jan Hus became disenchanted with the Latin Church, at least in some respects, and he too embarked upon a journey in search of truth and reform. His quest did not last a lifetime. Indeed, his exploration cost him his life.

---

[33] I have recently published a fulsome account of these events. Thomas A. Fudge, *Heretics and Politics: Theology, Power, and Perception in the Last Days of CBC* (Washougal, WA: Hewitt Research Foundation, 2014), 526pp.

CBC had prepared me well for introductory critical thinking. That was the harvest I gathered into the granary of my mind but CBC had not been an institution of intellectual depth, scholarship, or preparation for any proper investigation into the medieval world or historical theology. Hence, I was over my head shortly after the closure of CBC when I had a book called up from the closed stacks of the central branch of the Multnomah County Library. This was Matthew Spinka's monograph on Jan Hus' idea of the church.[34] This was a piece of proper scholarship. However, the prevalent use of many unpronounceable Czech names and other technical terminology created a psychological barrier through which I was quite unable to penetrate. I set Matthew Spinka aside with reluctance feeling that perhaps Jan Hus was too far removed from me, his medieval world too dissimilar to my own modern world and thus we were doomed never to meet properly. Hus tells us of a period in his own life when he, too, also possessed, what he characterized as, a very "weak intellect" but when this disability was eliminated he was able to deal more adequately with those matters of importance.[35] In the meanwhile, I too became a "backslider" from the "organization" and decided I could not any longer, even passively, give assent to the "message." After being a priest for a decade, Hus likewise arrived at a turning point in his own life when he openly and stridently began to dissent from the standards of authority and bluntly told his congregation from the pulpit that he would no

---

[34] Matthew Spinka, *John Hus' Concept of the Church* (Princeton: Princeton University Press, 1966).
[35] *Výklad na Páteř*, in MIHO, vol. 1, p. 342.

longer obey.[36] When I came to a crossroads in my own life pilgrimage, I undertook a major research investigation into the roots and beliefs of the "organization."[37] Don Fisher had directed me to find out the truth for myself, noting that while he could tell me what he thought truth was, it would do me little good. He told me that I had to make the discovery for myself.[38] This was a major turning point in my young intellectual journey. I had often knocked heads with Fisher, a powerful personality in his own right, and in many ways he seemed to bring out the worst in me, rebellion, anger, reckless thinking and the like, but this time I knew he was right and I was ready to accept his counsel and take up the challenge. I had no idea where that long and winding road would eventually lead and I also had no awareness of how far it would take me.

Hus had once observed with much regret that too many fled from the truth and lacked courage to defend truth. Hus admits that he too had once been numbered among that group and had not dared to speak openly and plainly on behalf of truth. Hus observed that some people were simply timid. Others feared loss of esteem or prestige. Still others desired the praise of those in high places. Others were quite fearful of losing their positions or being mocked, misunderstood, held in lasting contempt, persecuted, excommunicated, or forced to suffer

---

[36] Sermon preached on 20 December 1410. Text in Václav Flajšhans, ed., *Mag. Io. Hus Sermones in Capella Bethlehem, 1410-1411*, 6 vols. (Prague: České společnosti nauk, 1938-45), vol. 2, p. 202.

[37] Thomas A. Fudge, *The Historical Church and Modern Pentecostalism*, 1984, 116 page typescript.

[38] *The Journal of Thomas A. Fudge, 1980-1985*, entry for 19 September 1983.

bodily harm. Many people, Hus asserted, lacked the courage to risk their lives and thus they abandoned truth.[39] In the later Middle Ages, Hus was all too keenly aware of the high cost of conviction and the dangers in defending certain truths.

Fig. 14: John G. Diefenbaker, 1960s

I have thus far neglected to mention a man I never knew but one with whom I shared, along with Don Fisher, a common characteristic. That man was John G. Diefenbaker (1895-1979). Dief "the Chief," as he was fondly called, had been prime minister of Canada for six years between 1957 and 1963. It was said of John Diefenbaker, "show him the grain and he will go against it."[40] One of my CBC colleagues, David Brown, another Canadian, often talked about

---

[39] *O svatokupectví*, in MIHO, vol. 4, pp. 251-2.
[40] I later read his memoirs, John G. Diefenbaker, *One Canada: Memoirs of the Right Honourable John G. Diefenbaker*, 3 vols (Toronto: Macmillan, 1975-77). See also Denis Smith, *Rogue Tory: The Life and Legend of John G. Diefenbaker* (Toronto: Macfarlane Walter and Ross, 1995).

this aspect of Diefenbaker's personality. Don Fisher was also adverse to the well-worn grain and I came to recognize that I too was generally and similarly rather allergic to following the well-worn paths of the majority. The heretics caught my attention and Jan Hus especially began to beckon.

In 1348, Emperor Charles IV founded the first university in Central Europe, modelled directly on the University of Paris. Only the universities of Bologna, Paris, Oxford, and Cambridge are older than Charles University. Six centuries ago it was a thriving place where philosophers discussed the latest controversial ideas, a vibrant nascent reform movement was cultivated, and where theological debates reverberated from stone walls and echoed in the rooms of the fellows. The Karolina (or Charles College) is the oldest part of Prague University. Its Gothic window and silent gargoyles have witnessed the astute medieval schoolmen, the rise and fall of revolutions, foreign invasions, war, the shuttering of the whole place during World War Two, and the keen enthusiasm for unfettered thought and the establishment of an open marketplace for the free exchange of ideas following the momentous 1989 "Velvet Revolution." It was here, behind these old venerable stone walls, where the young Jan Hus became a critical thinker, a theologian, and prepared for his momentous career.

PART TWO

Perhaps my time at CBC was rather like Hus' schoolboy days in Prachatice. By 1986 I went on to Warner Pacific College which, in contrast to CBC, was a proper institution of higher learning, just as Hus had departed southern Bohemia, more than 600 years earlier and enrolled as a student at Charles

Fig. 15: Bronze relief of Jan Hus.
Bethlehem Chapel, Prague

University in Prague around 1390. By this time, I had made two important advances with respect to Jan Hus. The heady summer of 1984 had been spent wandering around Europe, reading some theology, visiting at least fourteen countries, working in a few academic libraries, and fully submerging myself in European culture and especially in the history of the Reformation. I did not work specifically on Hus, but I recall a visit to Worms, Germany where I spent a considerable amount of time observing the large and quite impressive Reformation monument there. Erected in 1868, the Worms memorial is reputedly the largest Reformation monument in the world. Martin Luther is the central figure towering above all the others. At his feet are the seated figures of Girolomo Savonarola and Jan Hus. Hus did not look much like Rod Colbin, but he was all I imagined he should be, wearing the cap of a scholar, bearded, and holding a crucifix. I still did not know much about him of any consequence. However, I was now more determined to gain meaningful acquaintance.

Founded in 1971, Powell's bookstore is one of the largest booksellers in the world. I have been going there since 1981 when Stan Johnson, then on the CBC staff, invited me to join him for a visit to the store. Powell's occupies 68,000 square feet of retail space which takes up an entire city block in downtown Portland. It claims an inventory of four million books. Open 365 days a year, I have spent a lot of time at Powell's and also spent a lot of money there. In the spring of 1985, now habitually unable to avoid Powell's for any length of time, I happened across a copy of a translation of Petr Mladoňovice's stirring account of the Hus trial at the Council of Constance. [41] It cost twenty-six dollars which was a tidy sum in those days but I knew I had to have it. I eagerly devoured the 300 pages and this time I was able to suppress my aversion to Czech names and soldier through the thickets of concepts which were still foreign to me. After carefully reading this text, I was even more committed to engaging with Jan Hus. However, I still required a mechanism to make that happen. That opportunity was just around the corner. Warner Pacific College provided the initial

---

[41] Matthew Spinka, *John Hus at the Council of Constance* (New York: Columbia University Press, 1965), pp. 87-234.

context in which to become a scholar of Hus and Hussite history.

In 1391, two men founded Bethlehem Chapel in Prague, a non-parochial chapel with a directive to feature sermons in the vernacular. The chapel was

Fig. 16: Bethlehem Chapel, Prague

raised on property owned by Václav Kříž in a large garden behind his house where the remains of an old malt-house stood. Conforming to the available space, the chapel was an irregular quadrangle with a massive pillar. One of the chapel founders made his intention quite clear in the foundation charter text. "I, Hanuš of Milheim ... have decided that this chapel will be named Bethlehem, which should be understood as the 'house of bread,' because I am convinced that common people and Christ's faithful should be fed there with the bread of the holy commandment."[42] The third preacher to occupy the

---

[42] The charter is dated 24 May 1391 and has been edited and published in Anton Dittrich, ed., *Monumenta historica*

pulpit was Jan Hus appointed to that position in 1402. Bethlehem Chapel is a large open space where 2,000 people can congregate. The pulpit can only be entered from a stairwell leading from an upper level of the old malt-house where, in the fifteenth century, the preacher resided. It was torn down in 1786 but excavations in the late 1940s revealed that two of the original medieval walls had been incorporated into other buildings. On one of the walls, beneath plaster, inscriptions placed there a half millennium earlier by Hus were uncovered.[43]

I shared an early interest in music with Hus. Much later, Hus tells us that "when I was a student, I sang vigils with others. However, we sang them as quickly as possible in order to finish the job as soon as we could."[44] The choirboy soon moved on to other things. Having abandoned my initial dream of music, I enrolled at Warner Pacific with a major in Religion. The WPC Department of Religion had a member of the faculty in those days who played a not-inconsequential role in my early work on Hus. Professor Irv Brendlinger was an expert on John Wesley with research interests in the antislavery movement. He taught courses both in theology and church history and I gravitated to these.

The summer of 1987 was spent on a small farm outside Canora, Saskatchewan with my friend Lynn Hennessy and her family. Here I occupied myself

---

universitatis Carolo-Ferdinandeae Pragensis, vol. 2 *Codex diplomaticus* (Prague: Spurny, 1834), pp. 300-308.

[43] Bohumil Ryba, *Betlemské texty* (Prague: Orbis, 1951). On the history and reconstruction of the chapel, along with many photographs, see especially Alois Kubiček, *Betlémská kaple*, second edition (Prague: Státní nakladatelství krásné literatury, hudby a umění, 1960).

[44] *Výklad na páteř*, in MIHO, vol. 1, pp. 346-7.

studying both the Hebrew Bible and John Calvin. A fortuitous finding in a Manitoba bookshop propelled me into Jan Hus once more and this time my interest and resulting research took lasting root and has persisted up to the present. During my stay in Saskatchewan, I drove over to Winnipeg, Manitoba

Fig. 17: Farm near Canora, Saskatchewan,
Canada, summer 1987

(a distance of about 300 miles) and flew to Boston to spend a few days with my parents, punctuated by numerous stops at book stores. On the return, I continued my usual habit of visiting used book shops. The only one I can recall in Winnipeg city is Highbrow Books, then located at 290 Bannatyne Avenue. I only know the address and name of the shop because the salesperson who took my twelve Canadian dollars and sold me a book placed a bookmarker inside. The place is still in business though it has shifted locations at least twice since I was there.[45] Notwithstanding this, I found a slender

---

[45] The shop currently has a location listed at 200 Provencher Blvd in Winnipeg, Manitoba Canada R2H 0G3. For details see

black volume on the shelves (a mere 103 pages) which immediately caught my eye, commanded my sustained attention, and demanded that I buy it. It was a hitherto unknown volume apparently written by the late medieval Italian humanist and book-hunter, Poggio Bracciolini and was an eyewitness

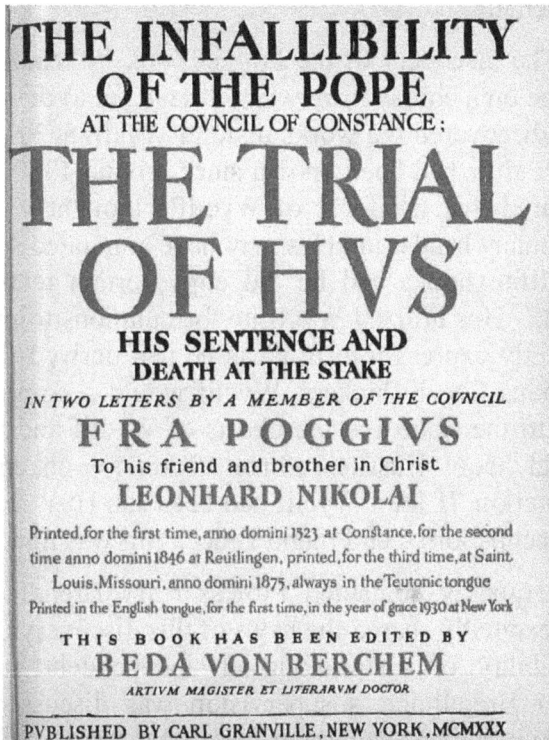

THE INFALLIBILITY OF THE POPE AT THE COVNCIL OF CONSTANCE; THE TRIAL OF HVS HIS SENTENCE AND DEATH AT THE STAKE IN TWO LETTERS BY A MEMBER OF THE COVNCIL FRA POGGIVS To his friend and brother in Christ LEONHARD NIKOLAI

Printed, for the first time, anno domini 1523 at Conſtance, for the second time anno domini 1846 at Reütlingen, printed, for the third time, at Saint Louis, Missouri, anno domini 1875, always in the Teutonic tongue Printed in the English tongue, for the first time, in the year of grace 1930 at New York

THIS BOOK HAS BEEN EDITED BY BEDA VON BERCHEM *ARTIVM MAGISTER ET LITERARVM DOCTOR*

PVBLISHED BY CARL GRANVILLE, NEW YORK, MCMXXX

Fig. 18: Titlepage of the alleged account
by Poggio Bracciolini

account of the Hus trial at Constance.[46] I read this book with keen eagerness and was soon convinced I had made a significant discovery. Even Spinka had

---

https://plus.google.com/110918424078934495290/about?gl=a u&hl=en
[46] Beda von Berchem, ed., *Hus the Heretic by Poggius the Papist* (New York: Carl Granville, 1930).

failed to refer to this source in his account of the trial of Jan Hus. I scanned the bibliographies and references of every book I had access to about Hus and came up empty. Not one single scholar seemed to know anything about this primary source. I was completely energized with enthusiasm and neophyte excitement.

The discovery of the Poggio book in Winnipeg set me on a course from which I have yet to deviate. Hus discovered the works of John Wyclif at Prague where they had been known since around 1380 and declared that the force of Wyclif's thought would turn many heads. Jan Hus may have annotated some Wyclifite books and he did copy certain texts in 1398.[47] Hus utilized Wyclifite formulations to more cogently express reform ideas he had derived from previous Czech thinkers. Wyclif would accompany Hus to the stake and the ghosts of Wyclif and Hus would haunt Hussite reform efforts for an entire generation. If John Wyclif had been Jan Hus' initial preoccupation, then Poggio Bracciolini was mine.

I quickly contacted Professor Irv Brendlinger and excitedly shared the news of this discovery. The possibility of undertaking an independent study under Brendlinger's supervision was discussed. I took up this opportunity in the winter term of 1988. I do not fear any misrepresentation in recalling that Dr. Brendlinger was also cautiously optimistic and shared my excitement. I did undertake, during the winter term of 1988, an investigation of the Poggio

---

[47] Václav Novotný, *M. Jan Hus Život a učení*, 2 vols (Prague: Laichter, 1919-1921), vol. 1, pp. 59-61 and František Šmahel, "'Doctor evangelicus super omnes evangelistas': Wyclif's Fortune in Hussite Bohemia" *Bulletin of the Institute of Historical Research* 43 (May, 1970), pp. 17-19.

document, though in truth I had been working away on the topic since the previous September. It was during this research project that I first spent a great deal of study time in the wonderful library at the admirably situated Mt. Angel Benedictine Abbey located less than forty miles south of Portland. My research into the Poggio text met with disastrous results. I discovered solid irrefutable grounds for excluding the authorship of Poggio Bracciolini or indeed of anyone else who may have been at Constance during the time of Hus. I also discovered, to my chagrin, that I was not the first to investigate Poggio or subject the text to an interrogation.[48] I was disappointed. I think I had imagined a headline in the *Oregonian* to the effect "WPC student makes profound discovery." I may have envisioned my photograph on the front page holding Poggio aloft triumphantly with a proud and smiling Professor Irv Brendlinger hovering in the background and Warner Pacific College now established on the international academic map. Alas, it was not to be. Nevertheless, I did produce a lengthy study of Hus' theology and that project, limited by all of the deficiencies and shortcomings typical of over-zealous and under-qualified college students, launched my career as a specialist on Jan Hus.[49] I learned two things from Irv Brendlinger which I have tried to emulate. The

---

[48] I uncovered two much earlier studies. David S. Schaff, "A Spurious Account of Huss's Journey to Constance, Trial, and Death" *The American Journal of Theology* 19 (No. 2, 1915), pp. 276-82, and Richard G. Salomon, "Poggio Bracciolini and Johannes Hus" *Journal of the Warburg and Courtauld Institutes* 19 (1956), pp. 174-7.

[49] Thomas A. Fudge, *"O Cursed Judas:" A Theological Study of the Heretic Master Jan Hus*, 1988, 143pp. This was accurately noted in an article "Warner Grad Becomes Religion Scholar," *WPC News* 11 (No. 2, Spring 1993), pp. 13-14.

first was high standards and a firm commitment to always striving to meet those standards. The other lesson learned, was his insistence that one should go, wherever possible, to the primary sources and not settle for dependence on secondary sources. Hus

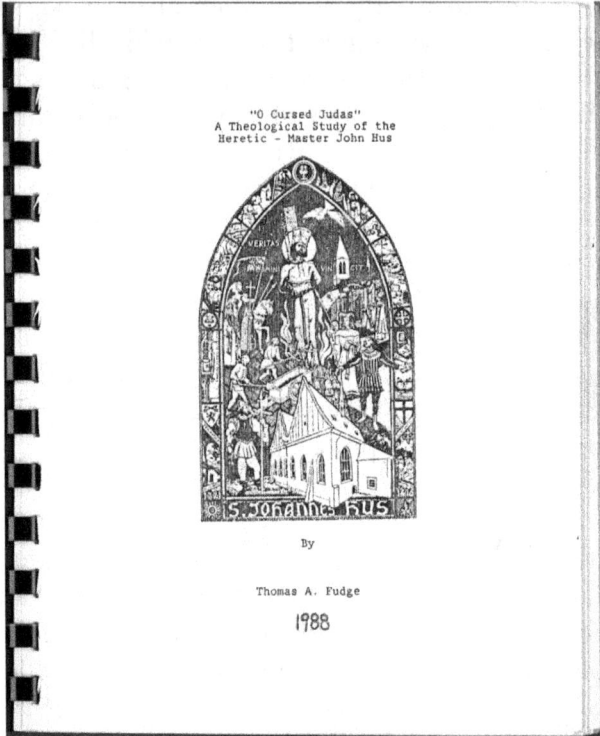

Fig. 19: First research project on Jan Hus, 1988

stoutly declared that "from the very beginning of my studies I made it a rule that whenever I encounter a sounder opinion to happily and humbly surrender the one previously embraced. For I am quite certain, just as Themistius says, that what we know is considerably less than what we do not know."[50] This is the proper stance for committed and serious scholars. Research is perilous and can expose one to confusion, doubt, anxiety, and, in religious terms, faith crises. Albert Schweitzer put it succinctly: "If thought is to set out on its journey unhampered, it must be prepared for anything, even for arrival at intellectual agnosticism."[51] Hus was never quite so brazen or bold. He never conceived of spiritual agnosticism, but he was quite prepared to risk it all, even life and limb, in the pursuit of truth. The true intellectual must be prepared to risk.

Originally located in the Lesser Town of Prague on the west bank of the Vltava River, the Hussites burned down the archbishop's palace in 1420. It was rebuilt later in the castle which towers over the Lesser Town and can be seen there to this day. The present structure dates from the sixteenth century. Jan Hus was a risk taker. This garnered him many great and powerful enemies. Chief among those detractors was Archbishop Zbyněk. Most people tend to buckle when called to the office of a man who reports directly to God's representative. Hus did not. When told that he was promoting heresies contained in the books of John Wyclif and ordered to surrender the offending materials, rather than meekly handing over his collection to the bonfire, Hus went to the archbishop and demanded to be shown chapter and verse of the alleged errors and heresies rumored to be contained within the said volumes. It is unlikely the appointed archbishop

---

[50] Noted in his treatise, *Defensio libri de Trinitate*, in MIHO, vol. 22, p. 42. Themistius was a fourth-century pagan teacher and philosopher active at Constantinople.

[51] Albert Schweitzer, *The Philosophy of Civilization*, part 1 *The Decay and Restoration of Civilization*, trans., C.T. Campion (New York: Macmillan, 1960), p. 63.

was sufficiently competent to assist Jan Hus in this matter. Hus had already written a book arguing that even tracts by heretics had value and should be read.[52] As the faggots were being gathered for the bonfire, Hus opposed the initiative from the pulpit of Bethlehem Chapel. Affronted and angry, Zbyněk ordered the immediate immolation of more than 200 volumes of John Wyclif's books. On 16 July 1410, Canon Zdeněk of Chrást ignited the fire behind the tightly closed, securely locked and guarded gates of the archiepiscopal courtyard. Throughout the city of Prague, massive outrage rocked the streets.[53]

During the same time as I was vainly striving to prove the veracity of Poggio's account of the Hus trial, during spring term 1988, I enrolled in a course on historiography which was taught by the young Professor Cole P. Dawson. Knowing of my work on Hus, Dawson magnanimously permitted me to use that topic for compiling a comprehensive annotated bibliography of Hus, which was one of the course requirements. I thought this would be a simple thing to accomplish inasmuch as I had been, for the previous six months, reading and researching Hus. I availed myself of a reference librarian at the nearby Western Conservative Baptist Seminary who took me step by step through an electronic database for journal articles dealing with Jan Hus. This was an entirely new research resource for me. I still recall coming up with about thirty-eight entries in all and also included two or three foreign–language sources which I thought would certainly impress Professor Dawson. At some point I conveyed to Dawson the

---

[52] See his treatise *De libris hereticorum legendis*, in MIHO, vol. 22, pp. 21-37.

[53] *Chronicon universitatis Pragensis*, in FRB, vol. 5, p. 572.

depth and breadth of my diligent research efforts. We were walking up the stairs on the south slope of Mt. Tabor, on the WPC campus, between Egtvedt Hall and A.F. Gray Hall, when I triumphantly informed Dawson that my exhaustive searches had revealed there were less than forty sources relating to Jan Hus. Dr. Dawson's caustic reply took me off guard when he scoffingly growled, "there has to be more than that!" I assured him there was not. He stalked away with a scowl. My self-assurance was dampened and I wondered what Dr. Dawson could possibly know that I didn't. After all, he was an historian of colonial America. Mildly offended by the dismissive attitude of my professor I decided to prove his comment incorrect. The main difficulty was that I encountered the unknown work of Jarold K. Zeman.[54] Zeman's catalogue listed a total of 3,853 items (on the wider topic of Hussites) and of that large number there were no fewer than 565 entries in the English language. While most of these focused on topics other than Jan Hus specifically, Zeman had proven Dawson right. I was remanded back to the library! The simple lesson I learned from Dawson was that in terms of proper historical research there is always more than meets the eye, "X" never, ever, marks the spot, and reliance on databases, or other artificial means, to do research is both misleading and perilous.

I left Warner Pacific College in 1988 and went on to graduate school having been awarded a full

---

[54] The work was Jarold K. Zeman, *The Hussite Movement and the Reformation in Bohemia, Moravia and Slovakia (1350-1650): A Bibliographical Study Guide (With Particular Reference to Resources in North America)* (Ann Arbor: University of Michigan Slavic Publications, 1977).

seminary scholarship to the Iliff School of Theology
in Denver, Colorado. Professors Irv Brendlinger and
Cole Dawson were instrumental in setting me more
firmly and more securely on my intended pathway
to productive research on Jan Hus. One of the first
things I did upon arrival in Denver was to order a

Fig. 20: Epiphany Lutheran Church, Denver, Colorado, 1990:
Peggy, Thomas, Joyce, and James Fudge

personal copy of Zeman's bibliographical study
guide from the Tattered Cover book shop which in
those days was a well-known Denver landmark.
This is a volume which has remained within arm's
reach for each of the past twenty-seven years. It is
somewhat worse for the wear and much has been
added to Zeman's work since 1977. Zeman became
a reference I have drawn upon repeatedly. I also
began a dimension of my work which persists to the
present. I began acquiring virtually everything I
possibly could on Hus and on early Hussite history.
I prioritized English-language studies and sources

and these formed the basis for my ongoing research. Between 1988 and 1992, I amassed a wide range of sources including books, book chapters, essays, book reviews, dictionary and encyclopedia entries, as well as Master's theses and PhD dissertations. By 1992, when I arranged to have my bibliographical collection typed up, I discovered it filled seventy pages. Dawson was right. When I went overseas to undertake a PhD, one of the items which went into the cargo hold was a metal trunk containing all of my collected papers. I recall the trunk weighed just under a hefty 130 pounds. I imagined Cole Dawson somewhere, out of sight, smirking. While studying at Iliff, I also served on the staff of the ELCA Epiphany Lutheran Church. At the same time, the incumbent Professor of Historical Theology and Church History at Iliff, Professor J. Alton Templin, gave me the opportunity to present two lectures on Hus and Hussite history in his introductory Church History course in the seminary. These were the first of many presentations on Hussite topics. While at Iliff seminary, I learned Latin and also undertook my beginning studies in the Czech language under the direction of Libor Brom (1923-2006). Brom was the Professor of Foreign Languages and Literatures and director of Russian Area Studies at the adjacent University of Denver. Brom was a Czech émigré who had arrived in America in 1948. Initially, he tried to persuade me to study Jan Amos Comenius, who had written only in Latin, and thereby avoid, what he described as, the difficult Czech language. He advised me that Czech was more difficult than Russian. But I was not to be deterred. I had no real interest in Comenius. Instead, I was determined to come to terms with Jan Hus. Brom relented.

Prague Castle is rooted in the Middle Ages with its foundations in the ninth century. The resplendent St. Vitus' Cathedral had been first established in the dark tenth century and the castle has witnessed the rise and fall of emperors and kingdoms, pretenders, two world wars, assassinations, revolts, clandestine coronations, and even the presence of popes. The

Fig. 21: St. Vitus' Cathedral, Prague Castle

Thirty Years' War was started because three men were defenestrated on the south slope. The daring vertical lines of the old cathedral, diamond-studded monstrances, centuries-old religious houses, and a presidential palace are only some of the features of this extraordinary place. I spent one entire and fulfilling summer in the Prague Castle, poring over medieval manuscripts in the deserted Cathedral Chapter Library in pursuit of the ever-elusive Hus. My early work with Libor Brom had been useful.

In 1989, I travelled to Chicago to attend the national conference of the (SBL) Society of Biblical Literature and the American Academy of Religion

(AAR), of which, at that time, I was a member. By this time, I was very enthusiastic about Hus and the prospects of undertaking post-graduate research in that area. One of my former college teachers, John Elias Stanley, bluntly told me in front of a number of other colleagues over lunch, "if you plan to go to Cambridge and write a dissertation on Hus, you will never get a job." The spouse of that sage professor chimed in with the admonition that I had best listen to the wise advice just offered. Hus had also been admonished. He was repeatedly warned that should he persist in adhering to John Wyclif he would get himself ever more deeply into serious trouble. Hus appeared deaf to such instruction. Jarold Zeman told me in 1995, in his strong Czech accent, that people would think I was "some sort of queer" if I persisted with my interests in Hus and his followers. I had not really thought about that, but Zeman was probably right. In the end, I did not care what people thought. Ultimately, I elected to place my loyalty firmly with the Diefenbaker doctrine rather than with the odd unsolicited Chicago opinion. Thus, in due course, I predictably, went to jolly old England and worked on Hussite history as my dissertation topic. It had not been an essay road. I had only been admitted to CBC a decade earlier with the proviso of academic probation. Based on my high school marks (which were utterly pathetic!), it was naturally uncertain if I had the required intellectual wherewithal to attend and successfully study at this non-accredited school sponsored by "the organization."[55]

After I had proven my mettle at CBC, I then encountered two additional problems when seeking

---

[55] Anne Wilkins, CBC Registrar, official letter of acceptance for admission to Thomas A. Fudge, 20 February 1981.

an appropriate doctoral-level supervisor. The small handful of Hussite experts in the Anglo-world were toiling mainly at institutions which did not offer the PhD. Generalists at larger institutions were reluctant to supervise. I believe, in hindsight, this was chiefly on account of the language barrier but also because of institutional prejudice against Hussites. The field of Reformation Studies is dominated by a western European bias. Earlier this year, I was contacted by a graduate student working at a very large and well-known American university. I cite the following extract from his letter: "No one at [this university] would likely support me as a PhD student since the faculty has largely sided with Luther as the 'victor' of the Protestant Reformation and really no one on the faculty - Religion and History, is interested in Bohemian history ... From my Reformation History professor, any attempt to study the Hussites would be career suicide - I would be unemployable." I have a file filled with curious rejection letters from academics situated all over the English-speaking world dating from the late 1980s. Twenty-five years does not seem to have changed attitudes. Affiliation with the suspected Wyclif in the fifteenth century was considered a liability for Jan Hus and intimate association with Hussites in the twenty-first century seems, at least in some quarters, to have adverse career implications. I advised the student to adopt the Diefenbaker doctrine.

The Charles Bridge, built in the 1350s, has been called the most beautiful bridge in all Europe. The bridge spans 679 yards long and is built on sixteen arches. It is protected by three bridge towers, two of them on the Lesser Quarter side and the third one on the Old Town side. The bridge is decorated by a continuous alley of thirty statues and statuaries. It is now a pedestrian bridge and though empty of motor vehicles it is routinely jammed with large crowds of tourists speaking two dozen languages and lined with venders catering to all manner of interest and industry. Before 1841, it was the only bridge across the Vltava River anywhere near Prague. Not once does Hus mention walking across the span but there

Fig. 22: Charles Bridge, Prague

is every reason to believe that he must have crossed the Vltava many times by means of the old bridge. I have been on the Charles Bridge in wind, rain, sun, and snow, by day and by night, following the faint footprints of Jan Hus.

In 1989, as I was contemplating doing the PhD, the former professor of systematic theology at Basel University, the Czech scholar Jan Milič Lochman (1922-2004), contacted me about the possibility of undertaking doctoral-level work with the Catholic theologian Hans Küng (1928-) at the University of Tübingen. At the time, Küng was a well-known and controversial thinker. In 1979, Pope John Paul II had formally banned Küng from teaching Catholic theology though he would remain at Tübingen for the balance of his career as Professor of Ecumenical Theology. At his official retirement in 1996, he was appointed Emeritus Professor. I corresponded with

Küng who expressed keen interest in Jan Hus and in the latter's doctrine of the church which Küng opined was perhaps not so radically different from his own ideas as articulated in one of his massive publications.[56] Küng thought it might be useful for a doctoral student to compare his understanding of the church, in the late twentieth century, with the ecclesiology of Jan Hus as expressed in the fifteenth century. I was definitely interested. After all, it was Hus' doctrine of the church which comprised the lion's share of the final indictment lodged against him at Constance. However, Küng thought the work should best be undertaken by a Roman Catholic. That disqualified me, though I was never clear why Küng assumed I was not of the Roman persuasion. Possibly my presumed association with Lochman was the telltale clue. Despite this setback, I soon thereafter did undertake a preliminary examination of the two ecclesiologies, which resulted in an essay which I then presented at an academic conference.[57] I had some additional contact with Hans Küng, but our conversations in 1989, and my short essay, were as close as I came to working with him at Tübingen.

My sustained efforts to secure a place at a first-rate institution eventually came to fruition and I was accepted for PhD studies both at the University of Toronto and at Cambridge University. I chose the

---

[56] The main text is Hans Küng, *The Church*, trans., Ray and Rosaleen Ockenden (New York: Sheed and Ward, 1967). This was the English version of his *Die Kirche* which had appeared the same year.

[57] Thomas A. Fudge, "The Church in the Shadow of Heresy: An Ecclesiological Analysis of Jan Hus' *De ecclesia* and Hans Küng's *Die Kirche*," unpublished paper, presented at the American Academy of Religion, regional conference, Denver, Colorado, 28 April 1990, 18pp.

latter. Had I gone to Toronto, I would have done my work under the supervision of Professor David R. Holeton, an Anglican priest and liturgical authority who had written his own PhD at the Sorbonne in Paris on the practice of infant communion within Hussite religious communities. Father Holeton and I became good friends and professional colleagues

Fig. 23: David R. Holeton, Prague, 2014

and have enjoyed a relationship which exists to the present. Holeton was quite clearly my earliest and most important colleague and for a number of years a source of great encouragement and support. Our relationship changed over the years as relationships tend to do. This was a matter of considerable regret. We did not suffer the sort of breach in friendship that Hus and his one-time friend Štěpán Páleč did. Eventually, however, we both had to sustain serious damage to our respective careers, though for quite different reasons. Still, I have always liked "Father David" and continue to regard him as a friend and respected colleague. He later agreed with me that I had made the better choice to go to Cambridge.

So I went up to Cambridge and here I came under the positive influence of Robert W. Scribner. Bob Scribner was not expert on things Hussite and

Fig. 24: Robert W. Scribner, Clare College,
Cambridge, c.1995

in fact had neither been to Prague nor had he seen the inside of a Czech archive. Nevertheless, he quite readily agreed to become my *Doktorvater* because he was not adverse to going against the grain. I was beginning to detect an intellectual pattern. Scribner was Australian, Roman Catholic, and a significant presence in the study of the German Reformation. Scribner was, in many respects, a perfect supervisor for me. He had left Sydney in 1967 and went to Germany intent upon undertaking doctoral level research on aspects one might generally now refer to as a social history of the Reformation. He was bluntly told by the all-wise German scholars of that period that there was no such topic. Adopting the essential Diefenbaker point of view, Scribner took absolutely no note of that questionable counsel. Instead, he simply migrated to London, came under the supervision of A.G. (Geoff) Dickens and wrote his PhD dissertation on that topic anyway, based on extensive work in archives in Erfurt, of all places.[58]

There were few western scholars working in east German archives in those Cold War days, but the alien-outsider Scribner accomplished what he had been warned was quite impossible, undoable, and which, according to the over-confident and all-knowing German historians, totally failed to even qualify as a legitimate line of inquiry. By 1996, Bob had taken up a chair at Harvard but died shortly thereafter. At the time of his untimely death at age fifty-six, in 1998, Scribner had emerged as arguably the leading international authority on the social history of the Reformation, best known widely for his seminal and stimulating work on popular visual images.[59] At my important and formal confirmation

---

[58] "Reformation, Society and Humanism in Erfurt c.1450-1530," 2 vols., PhD thesis, University of London, 1972.

[59] R.W. Scribner, *For the Sake of Simple Folk: Popular Propaganda for the German Reformation*, 2nd edition (Oxford: Clarendon Press, 1994). Originally published by Cambridge University Press in 1981.

of candidature hearing at Cambridge, following two terms of work, I was told on that occasion by the chatty and opinionated Peter Burke, currently the Professor Emeritus of Cultural History and longtime Fellow of Emmanuel College at Cambridge, that it appeared to him that I was attempting to do for fifteenth-century Bohemia what Bob Scribner had already done for sixteenth-century Germany. To say the least, I was somewhat more than merely a little intrigued by Burke's parallel. Later news of Bob's death came as a blow and there has hardly been a day that goes by that I do not think of poor old Bob and wonder what all he might have accomplished, brilliant thinker and first-rate historian that he was, had he been able to enjoy a full career.

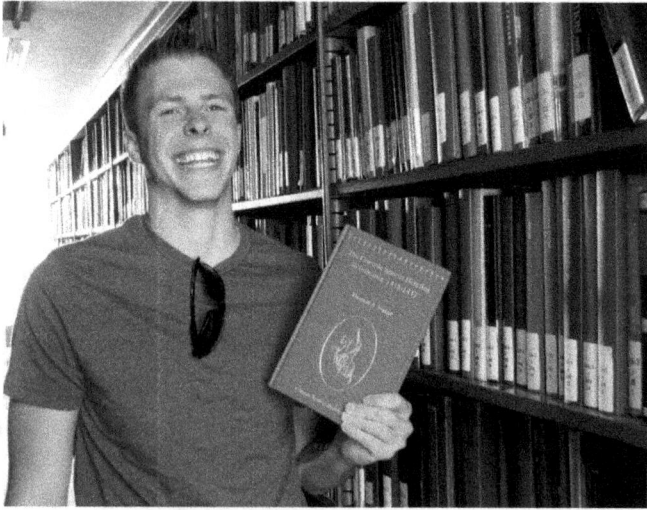

Fig. 25: Jakoub Luther Fudge, finding one of his father's books. Cambridge University Library, June 2011

My first meeting with Scribner in his rooms at Clare College ended with a request that I submit to him a list of all the sources and scholarship I had already read. I promptly produced a thirty-five page bibliography. Scribner then adjudicated that I had already, effectively, completed the first year of doctoral studies. Somewhere on the other side of the Atlantic, I could see Dr. Cole Dawson smiling and saying, "Fudge, I told you there had to be more!" With the preliminary work already done, Scribner sent me off to spend the requisite time working in continental archives. For me, this meant Prague and Vienna. I remember the first time I saw a highway sign reading "Prag." This was somewhere in the former East Germany, commonly referred to in the west in the old cold-war days as the DDR (Deutsche Demokratische Republik), as I was on my way to south Poland. All these years later, I can still recall the excitement of getting near to the place where Hus had spent the bulk of his career.

The hills and fields of Bohemia are drenched in blood, sweat, and tears. Just west of Prague, for example, is the White Mountain, where a decisive battle was waged and won which set the stage for the seventeenth-century Thirty Years' War. There are fields that are empty and nameless and lives that were lost there now long forgotten and gathered into the kingdoms of the dead. There are ghosts and spirits, history and mystery, and even though the medieval knights no longer joust, there are furrows unseen and unknown which laid the foundations for ideas and civilizations. Even some of the locals have forgotten or perhaps never knew the secrets in the fields so near. In one instance, twenty-five years ago, I had to argue and cajole to convince a native Czech that down this road and across that field lay the house where history was made. He doubted. I insisted. We found it.

The road ahead was still not going to be easy. I encountered banned books catalogues in Prague, the oppressive and irritating dead hand of Communist Czechoslovakia, hopelessly inaccessible archives, puzzled librarians and archivists who could simply not understand why someone from faraway Canada had come to Prague interested in the religious history of their country. Somewhere in those heady years, I encountered the perplexing problem of the year zero, the principle of the foul ball, along with a paradox which has remained stubbornly unrelieved. Clarity refused to emerge for another long decade until I met Franz Bibfeldt.[60] I persevered. There is

Fig. 26: The Committee for Resolving the Problem of the Year Zero: Irv Brendlinger, Franz Bibfeldt, Thomas A. Fudge, and Yern Yadon

one story which seems to be a fitting example of the circuitous pathway I had to follow in my journey between reading Bainton's *Here I Stand* at the age of fourteen to a more serious engagement with Hus. The story begins prosaically at a United Methodist seminary in Denver and ends rather dramatically at the Vatican in Rome.

---

[60] The authoritative and definitive study of Bibfeldt remains Martin E. Marty and Jerald C. Brauer, eds., *The Unrelieved Paradox: Studies in the Theology of Franz Bibfeldt*, second edition (Grand Rapids: Eerdmans, 2013).

One of the librarians at Iliff, knowing of my interest in the religious history of eastern Europe, contacted me concerning a new acquisition.[61] I was intrigued especially with a four page appendix to one of the chapters. The appendix listed sixty-one propositions and statements allegedly uttered by Hungarian Hussites in 1435 and reported to curial authorities by the inquisitor for the vicariate of Bosnia, Giacomo della Marca. Keeping in mind, Irv Brendlinger's admonition about primary sources, I set off to track down the inquisitor's report. There was no trace of it at Cambridge so I went to the renowned Bodleian Library in Oxford. Here I came across references, but not the text itself. Inasmuch as the content of the report related to Bohemia, I felt confident the document would come to light in Prague. I was quite amazed to find that none of the scholars I spoke to there, knew anything about it. I began to fear and suspect another Poggio deception. Drawing a blank in Prague, I took the next logical step which was to travel to Budapest. The document had originated in the historic lands of Hungary. Once again, I was disappointed to find no trace or knowledge of the report. It was put to me by József Török, a chain-smoking Hungarian scholar, that the report was probably in Rome. I had now either to admit defeat or press on to Rome. I opted for the latter and made my way down to the Eternal City. I appeared before the Vatican Library on a very hot summer day and was told quite firmly I could not be granted admission on the simple grounds that I was inappropriately attired. Anticipating this roadblock I

---

[61] Alexander Sándor Unghváry, *The Hungarian Protestant Reformation in the Sixteenth Century under the Ottoman Impact* (Lewiston: The Edwin Mellen Press, 1989). I was very interested in the content of pp. 106-109.

had come warned and prepared and my appearance
was immediately remedied. Thus, having passed the
clothesline test, I was ushered into a face to face
audience with the Prefect of the Vatican Library,
the Irish-Canadian scholar, the very well-known
Father Leonard Boyle (1923-1999), a member of
the Dominican Order, who was sometimes referred
to as "God's librarian." I had in my hand a brief

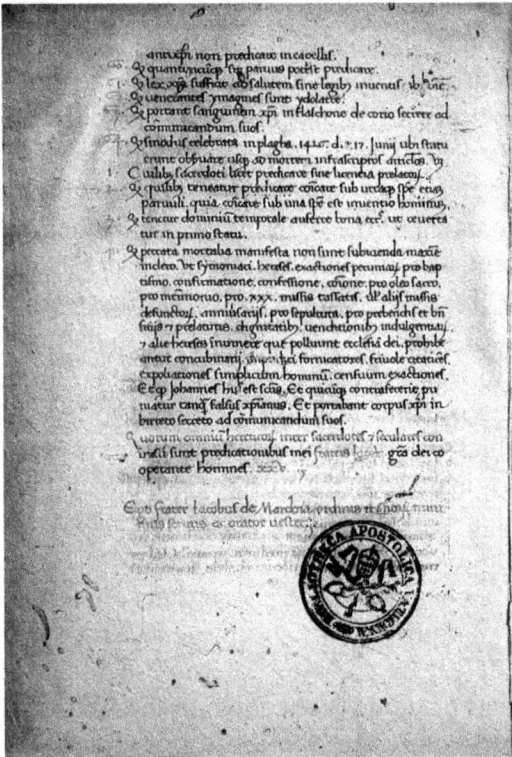

Fig. 27: The elusive fifteenth-century codex Vat Lat 7307

handwritten letter of introduction from David R.
Holeton, whom I had consulted in Prague, outlining
my inquiry and lending a modicum of support for
the legitimacy of my work. After reading the letter,
I was dismayed when Father Boyle politely asked

me why I thought the document might be within his purview. He told me that while I was in the Vatican Library, there was also the Vatican Archives, the curiously named Secret Archives, and two or three other quite separate and independent repositories each housed within the vast Vatican City complex. Sensing my acute disappointment he asked if by any chance I happened to have a manuscript shelf mark for the document I sought. When I announced that I did and said it aloud he promptly replied that the number was a Vatican Library manuscript and he would have it called up forthwith. In short order, I was finally, at last, holding in my hands the elusive fifteenth-century document relating to my ongoing research.[62] A few months later, while staying with David Holeton in Charlbury, a small village about eighteen miles northwest of Oxford, I undertook to transcribe parts of the manuscript which contained relevant material about Jan Hus.

Linden trees can reach 130 feet in height. Their trunks are very sturdy and they feature heart-shaped leaves. They provide deep shade and some of the linden trees in Europe have lasted over 1,000 years. The symbolic tree of the Czech Republic is a linden and the largest living tree in the country is also a linden, with a trunk perimeter of forty-one feet, in the tiny village of Pastviny near Ústí nad Orlici. The oldest linden tree is in the Iron Mountains (Železné Hory) in eastern Bohemia and is thought to have been there for a millennium. Jan Hus tells us that "previously I preached in towns and in the markets but now I preach among the hedges, in villages,

---

[62] Rome, Vatican Library MS Vat Lat 7307, fols. 23r-24v.

castles, fields, in the forests as well as beneath a linden tree at Kozí Castle."[63]

The several months in which I spent laboring in the many archives were extremely challenging, very fruitful, and even exciting. In the summer of 1991, in the company of my friend and colleague Tomáš Votava, I was able to visit more than fifty sites within Bohemia relating to Jan Hus and the early history of the Hussites. My regular communiqués dispatched to Scribner back in Cambridge indicated to him I was making excellent progress. Dining one

Fig. 28: With Blanka Šmídlová at "U koleje" restaurant in Prague, c.2000

---

[63] Text in František Palacký, ed., *Documenta Mag. Joannis Hus vitam, doctrinam, causam in constantiensi concilio actam et controversias de religione in Bohemia annis 1403-1418 motas illustrantia* (Prague: Tempsky, 1869), pp. 728-9 and *Postil*, in MIHO, vol. 2, pp. 320 and 378-9.

evening in a small Prague restaurant with my Czech friend Blanka Šmídlová, a casual comparison was drawn between me and my subject. Blanka told the waiter, a young man named Martin, about my work and my interest in Jan Hus. Martin looked at me intently for a moment and then said, "you look like Jan Hus. I hope you do not come to the same end." It was a throwaway comment and I took little note of it beyond a passing amusement. Meanwhile, with trips to Vienna, Basel, Rome, Göttingen, Budapest, London and Oxford, Edinburgh, countless places in the former Czechoslovakia, including the Czech National Library, the National Museum Library and the Prague Castle Archives, I completed my work and headed back to Cambridge University to write up the required dissertation.

During the writing up of my assembled research I had occasion to meet Malcolm Lambert. He had just retired from the University of Bristol and was best known for his work on medieval heresy which at that very moment was being revised for a second edition.[64] He had taken early retirement in order to devote himself more fully to other research interests including a re-examination of the Cathar heresy. Lambert suggested we meet at the Oxford Union, the well-known debating society situated in Oxford. I agreed. Lambert said he would bring along a copy of his *Medieval Heresy* book and by that sign I would be able to easily recognize him at the Oxford Union. As it turned out, there was no chance I could overlook Malcolm Lambert or mistake someone

---

[64] Since that time, the book has subsequently gone into a third edition under the title Malcolm Lambert, *Medieval Heresy: Popular Movements from the Gregorian Reform to the Reformation*, 3rd edition (Oxford: Blackwell, 2002).

else for him. When I entered the Oxford Union, at precisely the appointed time, I immediately noted a man walking back and forth at a prominent place holding aloft a copy of Lambert's *Medieval Heresy* above his head. I concluded this had to be Malcolm Lambert. My assumption was correct. Lambert, his wife and I took lunch at the Oxford Union and enjoyed a lengthy and stimulating discussion about heresy and Hussites. My other abiding memory of Lambert from our meeting at the Oxford Union was the peculiar fact that Lambert had a very long, dark, and thick patch of hair growing directly out of his nose extending halfway down to his upper lip. To this day I recall the nose-hair more clearly than I do his thoughts on Hus. I was also unaware at the time that Lambert and I would soon meet again under more formal circumstances.

During my research in continental archives, the focus of my work had shifted from Hus to some of his followers and in the end I produced a thick "book" of 465 pages outlining in detail my findings and conclusions.[65] I successfully defended my work during a two hour long oral defense (the traditional viva) convened at Queens' College in Cambridge which I arrived at by means of crossing the famous Mathematical Bridge. Here I encountered Malcolm Lambert once again. The viva included a somewhat heated head-to-head debate with Lambert, who was the external examiner and acknowledged authority on medieval heresy. Lambert strenuously objected

---

[65] Thomas A. Fudge, "Myth, Heresy and Propaganda in the Radical Hussite Movement, 1409-1437," PhD dissertation, 1992. It was described as "three and a half inches thick" in the article "Warner Grad Becomes Religion Scholar," p. 13. The description was a slight exaggeration.

to a statement I had included in my dissertation. This offending sentence stated that "heresy was the purely arbitrary invention of the medieval church." Lambert demanded and adamantly insisted that it be excised. I elected to argue the point. After a spirited debate lasting more than twenty minutes, I agreed to delete the word "purely" only. The exchange was great fun, even if somewhat risky. When Jan Hus was admonished to surrender the dangerous books in his personal library which had been written by John Wyclif, he did not passively comply with that formal episcopal order. Instead, he demanded to be shown why those particular books were considered to be so offensive and unacceptable. Hus' posture served as another valuable lesson.

After that culminating Cambridge event, I went directly to Portland, to take up my first academic appointment at my old *alma mater*, Warner Pacific College, replacing my friend and early mentor, Irv Brendlinger, who had recently resigned. My work at Cambridge had convinced me of one very important point which was that Jan Hus was not a Protestant. I was now convinced that it was fruitless to attempt to understand the meaning of Hus through the prism of Martin Luther, John Foxe, Matthias Flacius, *the* Reformation, or in any other way, save through his own work and in his own context. I had begun my work in the wider field of Reformation Studies but had concluded my doctoral research as a confirmed medievalist, though admittedly now occupying the *terra incognita* of the fifteenth century, a veritable frontier context which both medievalists and early modernists have routinely tended to avoid, being imprisoned in the artificial periodization created by historians.

The Gothic Church of the Mother of God before Týn dates to the fourteenth century. Its towers reach a height of eighty meters (263 feet). For more than

Fig. 29: The Church of Our Lady Before Týn, Prague, 14th century

two centuries it was a center of Hussite religion. In 1626, a gold chalice which formerly sat between the towers was removed, melted down, and replaced with a sculpture of the Virgin Mary. Jan Hus would have passed before this church in the main square of the Old Town in Prague countless times. Sometimes it is not an easy task to identify those elements or influences which exert formative pressure on our thinking. Much of it is unconscious like context, environment, social structures, and dominant mores which are taken for granted.

My father, Revd. James G. Fudge, Don Fisher, C.H. Yadon, and Irv Brendlinger were among those who had exerted significant influence on me from different angles and in different ways. Intellectually, there were several others who were also powerful influences on me. Three of them were men I never knew. The first is Martin Luther. If his work acted like a high-powered drill on the multiple religious worlds of sixteenth-century Europe, his thought and ideas also profoundly altered my own theological

Fig. 30: Martin Luther (1483-1546). Bronze statue located on the south side of the main entrance of the Market Church, Hannover, Germany

perspective. Martin Luther delivered me from the bondage of "the organization" and from the tyranny of "the message." His commentary on Galatians, his short tract on *The Freedom of a Christian*, his crisp and compelling articulation of justification by faith, his penetrating understanding of the eucharist, and his firm insistence on the centrality of the lordship of Christ, presented arguments I was wholly unable to resist.[66] By contrast, most of the Lutherans whom

---

[66] As an undergraduate at Warner Pacific, I wrote a term paper on Luther's understanding of faith, later developed and, after

I have known are not really Lutheran at all, in my opinion. I recall Gary M. Simpson, then senior pastor at the Lutheran Church of the Resurrection in Portland, but now professor of systematic theology at Luther Seminary in St. Paul, Minnesota, visiting my home around 1987 and our conversation on that occasion about Luther. Simpson was impressed that I owned all fifty-five volumes of the red American edition of Luther's Works (proudly displayed in my office) and also that I had read a great deal of them. I remember him saying he wished Lutherans would actually read Luther. He was further impressed with my story of how Martin Luther had shaped my own theology. My intense study of Luther had produced profound religious and intellectual transformation in my life. Had I not ultimately decided for Jan Hus, I would have become a passionate scholar of Luther.

The second influence was Roland H. Bainton. It was not just his engaging book on Luther but his whole approach to history and the liveliness of his prose which attracted me perhaps more than any other scholar. I have often wondered what it might have been like to have studied with Bainton who was, for forty-two years, the widely respected and renowned Titus Street Professor of Ecclesiastical History at Yale University. Bainton caused history to vividly come alive. He had that uncanny ability to capture the complexity of the past and cogently

---

several iterations over two decades, subsequently published. Thomas A. Fudge, "Saints, Sinners and Stupid Asses: The Place of Faith in Luther's Doctrine of Salvation" *Communio viatorum* 50 (No. 3, 2008), pp. 231-56. Both Irv Brendlinger and David W. Lotz, the latter at the time being the Washburn Professor of Church History at Union Theological Seminary in New York City, were influential inasmuch as both had taught stimulating courses on Luther in which I was a participant.

convey it in the present in a manner that was both penetrating and engaging. After my preoccupation

Fig. 31: Roland H. Bainton (1894-1984). Portrait by Deane Keller, 1975, Yale University Art Gallery

with *Here I Stand*, a copy of which I took with me to CBC, I made a specific point over the years to collect as many of Bainton's books as I could.

The third major influence was Matthew Spinka. He was significant chiefly for the sheer weight of his scholarship which was unparalleled in English. In my early days, Spinka was my guide to Hus and I absorbed his understanding and interpretation of Jan Hus. Spinka reflected a modern perspective not unlike that of the sixteenth-century martyrologist Matthias Flacius Illyricus with an unvarnished view of church history which clearly imagined Jan Hus as a recurring phoenix arising from the smouldering ashes of persecution and in that process reviving the moribund purity of the ancient faith. Hence, Spinka

Fig. 32: Matthew Spinka (1890-1972)

developed an interpretive model wherein Jan Hus became a veritable forerunner figure who bridged a transitional stage between the Middle Ages and the Reformations.[67] I would later untangle myself, to large extent, from Matthew Spinka's influence but the intellectual debt remained nonetheless.

The fourth influence was Robert Scribner, my Cambridge University *Doktorvater*, whom I have

---

[67] For example, Spinka, *John Hus' Concept of the Church*, p. 3 and Spinka, *John Hus: A Biography*, p. 3.

mentioned earlier, who exemplified scholarly rigor, endless probing questions, relentless methodology, a willingness to go against the grain, and a man who simply did not shy away either from history or its evidence. He likewise quietly convinced me to take seriously the visual sources of history. Behind his back at Cambridge, and out of earshot, I used to refer to Scribner as "Reader Bob," an allusion to his academic rank as "Reader." My PhD colleague Ken Marcus (now a professor at La Verne University in California) always found the moniker humorous but I always maintained a high level of respect for Bob.

The fifth influence was Jiří Kejř who had gained an impressive reputation as an expert on medieval canon law. I first met Kejř in 1991 at his home in

Fig. 33: With Jiří Kejř (1921-2015)
at Slavia, in Prague, 2010

Prague. We were to meet many times over the next two decades and from time to time there was also correspondence. It was his work as a legal specialist which caused me to rethink the trial of Hus and ultimately change my mind about Hus' treatment at

Constance.[68] Kejř once told me that apart from his beloved Prague, his favorite places in all the world were Cambridge, Assisi, and Constance. All five of these men are now deceased. In quite different ways, they were all good friends over many years, intellectual travelling companions, and each one is remembered with fondness in the words written by the nineteenth-century American Quaker poet John Greenleaf Whittier: "O calm of hills above, where Jesus knelt to share with thee, the silence of eternity."[69]

PART THREE

By 1412, Hus had been subjected to a total of four writs of official excommunication. Traditional ceremonies accompanied the formal eviction of one from the community of the faithful. The writ of excommunication against Jan Hus ordered abbots, priors, and all priests everywhere in every church, chapel and monastery, to intone a solemn mass. Following the liturgy, the ritual of excluding one from the household of pure faith should be carefully observed. The components of this rite included the ringing of a bell and the lighting of a candle, which

---

[68] There were many studies but by far the most important was his specific analysis of the trial process itself. Jiří Kejř, *Husův proces* (Prague: Vyšehrad, 2000) which I read very carefully and which I found to be almost entirely convincing as well as providing confirmation for my own conclusions which had been reached independently.

[69] The 1872 poem was adapted by Garrett Horder in 1884 into the well-known hymn "Dear Lord and Father of Mankind." Ian C. Bradley, *Abide With Me: The World of Victorian Hymns* (Chicago: GIA Publications, 1997), p. 171.

was quickly extinguished and knocked to the floor. A cross was raised, feet stomped the floor, spitting ensued, a door was closed, and three stones were thrown at the house of the excommunicate. This was the medieval ritual of bell, book, and candle.[70]

Hus lived in the shadow of the end of history, or at least an active expectation that the consummation of time was near. Each Christian generation for two thousand years has included a coterie of believers living in hope of cosmic transformation. On one occasion, I was working in the manuscripts reading room in the National Library in Prague poring over some obscure medieval text. David Holeton was also studying another text seated at the same table. Suddenly the archivist, a scholar by the name of Zdeněk Uhlíř, appeared at our table and solemnly announced in doleful tones, "in twenty minutes, it is the end!" Startled, Holeton and I looked up with quizzical expressions. Sensing our confusion, Uhlíř emphatically exclaimed, "at six o'clock, everything is all over!" We were now completely baffled and our faces must have suggested to Uhlíř a serious double case of mental deficiency. David looked at me, and I stared at him, and together we looked back at Uhlíř who was now annoyed with the daft scholars. He became agitated, slapping his wrist somewhat exaggeratedly. All at once the penny dropped: the time was 5:40 p.m. The archivist was

---

[70] On this, see especially Genevieve Steele Edwards, "Ritual Excommunication in Medieval France and England, 900-1200," PhD dissertation, Stanford University, 1997. A number of these components can be found specifically enumerated in the writ of excommunication against Hus announced by Zbyněk (*Documenta*, p. 399) and are present as well in the legal writ of excommunication later issued by Cardinal Peter Stephaneschi in *Documenta*, p. 463.

attempting to communicate that the manuscripts reading room would soon be closing for the day at 6:00 p.m. It was not the end of the world after all as we initially feared and there was also no impending catastrophe. What a relief! It had been a close call.

Fig. 34: Kozí Hrádek, south Bohemia

In the aftermath of his excommunication, Hus left Prague to spare the city the ravages of interdict. He returned to south Bohemia, to his roots, to the environment from whence he had come. Not far from what is today the city of Tábor, Hus was sheltered by sympathizers at the small Gothic castle of Kozí Hrádek (Goat Castle). Burnt down in 1438, it now lies in ruins in the midst of a forest. Some of the rooms are still identifiable and in one of these, Hus composed some of his most important works, including a treatise on the church. The moat is now dry. The original drawbridge is long gone. All of the rooms are airy, and the floors are covered with a carpet of grass. Many of the tourists who come to Kozí today are probably unaware that within these ruins, for more than a year and a half, a man whose name will live forever, once wrote important books, wandered in the nearby forest, preached sermons, and prepared for his final conflict.

It was during the two years I served on the Warner Pacific College faculty in PDX that my first formal publications on Hussite history occurred. As Charles Dickens wrote, it was the best of times, it was the worst of times. I had been an active part of a college faculty writers group. We used to meet weekly off campus. For a myriad of reasons, we

Fig. 35: The "Inept Group," Portland, c.1995:
Dan Cole-McCullough, Dennis Plies, Steve Arndt,
Lou Foltz, Cole Dawson

jokingly referred to ourselves as the "Inept Group." After my departure from the college, these men insisted I maintain my membership at the weekly meeting. They will never know how important that contact was during a very dark period of life. They were also good enough to read and comment on some of my early draft essays on Jan Hus. The premature termination of my work at Warner, sent me into exile in the south Pacific. My colleague and fellow "Inept" group member, Professor Louis G. Foltz sent me off with a handmade card expressing anticipation at the eventual production of a "Māori Hus." In due time I complied with that vision but it

Fig. 36: Louis G. Foltz, "The Māori Hus", 1995.
Hand drawing

required many more years than I imagined. If Hus had to endure exile in rural castles in the south and west of medieval Bohemia, my banishment required my presence in the modern antipodes.

If Warner Pacific afforded me the opportunity to become established as a teacher at the tertiary level, then during a busy nine years as a member of the History faculty at the University of Canterbury in Christchurch, on the south island of New Zealand, I was provided with the means of ample opportunity and funding to develop my interests in the legacy of Jan Hus and thus establish myself as a scholar. My appointment in the antipodes was made partly on the strength of Scribner's recommendation as well as his reputation. Bob's work was well-known and highly regarded at Canterbury. Some of my future colleagues believed I might be able to extend the

Scribnerian influence while my interests in eastern European history in the medieval and early modern periods was also compelling to the committee who interviewed me. Rumors that I had singlehandedly

Fig. 37: University of Canterbury,
Department of History, 2002

taught myself the difficult Czech language were both curious and much exaggerated. What about Libor Brom? During those mainly happy years at Canterbury, I taught a year-long Honours course on Jan Hus and Hussite history while establishing an ongoing productive research profile complete with commensurate publications. My first two books on Hussite history appeared, along with chapters in six other books and at least twenty-one articles in scholarly journals.[71] Neither book was specifically about Hus and only five of the other publications dealt in detail with him. However, I had actively continued reading Hus, thinking about him, and

---

[71] Thomas A. Fudge, *The Magnificent Ride: The First Reformation in Hussite Bohemia* (Aldershot: Ashgate, 1998) and *The Crusade against Heretics in Bohemia, 1418-1437* (Aldershot: Ashgate, 2002).

preparing for the focused work I eventually hoped to produce about him.

After a time at Kozí Hrádek, Hus was obliged to seek shelter elsewhere. He was offered a place in another fourteenth-century castle, this time west of

Fig. 38: Krakovec Castle, western Czech Republic

Prague at a place called Krakovec which still stands in ruins. Time was now running out for Jan Hus. In 2011, a sculpture of Hus, clean shaven and rotund, sitting in meditation, holding a book to his heart, was placed on a steep slope below the ruined ramparts of the old castle. From this place, Hus eventually travelled west, across the frontier out of Bohemia, and into a future fraught with peril and uncertainty. It is not possible to know what he thought, if he cast a backward glance at the old castle, as he rode westward into the sinking sun. Beyond the Šumava (the Bohemian Forest) were the German lands and his last opportunity to convince the church and the entire world that he was right and, much more importantly, to keep his date with destiny. Unfortunately, my own career experienced a near-disastrous interruption and for eight-and-a-half years I was in the academic wilderness. It was during this time of solitude that I was commissioned to write a book on Jan Hus. This proved to be the first of four volumes devoted entirely to Hus.[72]

Practically the one thing everyone knows about Hus is that he was burned at the stake. They may not know why, or when, or any of the particulars but his gruesome death stands out perhaps for its barbarity and the grotesque spectacle it embedded in the historical records. The burning of Master Jan Hus occurred in an altogether lovely place. The Bodensee is one of the largest lakes in Europe and is mentioned in historical records dating back to the mid-first century of the Common Era. Bounded by Switzerland, Austria and Germany, Lake Constance is both strikingly beautiful as well as historic. There is some possibility that Hus arrived at the Council via ship which he may have boarded in what is today Friedrichschafen. In view of the lake, Hus had also to face Latin Christendom. Hus faced his own stake. He could have recanted. He could have saved his life. He could have lived. But at what cost? The cost for life was conscience. The price to pay for avoiding the stake was perjury. Jan Hus refused. The Prague waiter Martin told me in 1991 he hoped I would not finish my life as Hus did. So far I had

---

[72] These were Thomas A. Fudge, *Jan Hus: Religious Reform and Social Revolution* (London: I.B. Tauris, 2010), *The Memory and Motivation of Jan Hus, Medieval Priest and Martyr* (Turnhout: Brepols, 2013), *The Trial of Jan Hus: Medieval Heresy and Criminal Procedure* (New York: Oxford University Press, 2013), and *Jan Hus Between Time and Eternity: Reconsidering a Medieval Heretic* (Lanham, MD: Lexington Books, 2016).

avoided the pyre. But, I did have my own stake a dozen years later. I could have walked away. I, too, could easily have recanted. I could have begged

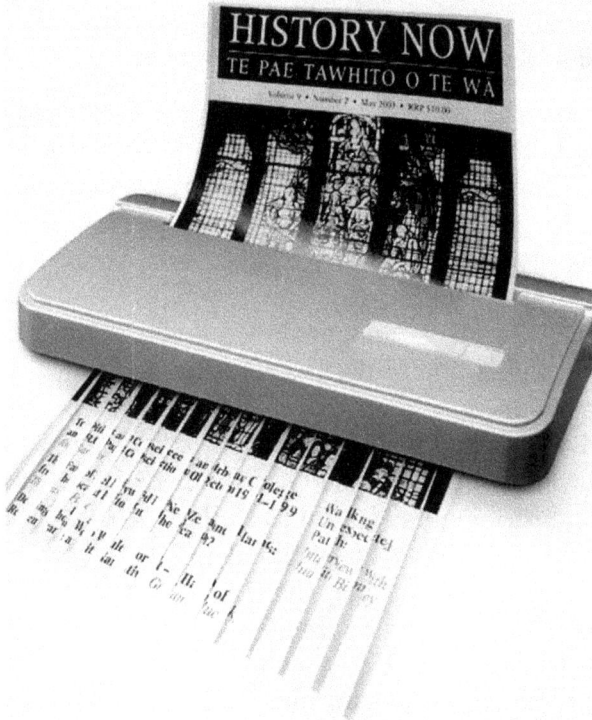

Fig. 39: Censorship at the University of Canterbury, 2003

forgiveness. I could have kept my pen in my pocket and kept my mouth shut. But at what cost? The price for silence was another man's professional life. The price to pay for that smoother career path was accepting intellectual terrorism. I refused to buckle. I do not believe Hus was a hero for going to the stake. I was no hero for defending academic principle. Hus did what he had to do and for that conviction and allegiance to truth he paid with his life. I did what I had to do and for that commitment

I spent almost nine years in the empty wilderness. But there is an important caveat to be made. There is a wide world of difference between the stake at Constance and a modern exile into the academic wilderness. If a parallel exists at all, it does so only in terms of attempting to do the right thing for the right reason. In consequence, my own career as an academic and as a university professor was almost destroyed. I applied for a total of 261 academic jobs and received 261 rejection letters. Book burning in the fifteenth century was replicated by the Nazis in 1933 and had now become essay shredding in the early twenty-first century at the hands of modern academics. What a predicament! Over the years I had amassed a large personal scholarly library of 8,000 volumes. During the years in the wilderness, I used to ruefully tell visitors that my personal library represented the man I had once aspired to be. I have no reason to doubt that Hus regretted his decision. For me, like Edith Piaf's well-known and famous signature song, "Non, je ne regrette rien", there are no regrets. However, there are consequences.

In 1416, a Hussite priest announced that "three [men] were decapitated publicly in front of a large crowd in Prague, in the faith of the blessed Trinity, joyful and with cheerful faces."[73] He was referring to three young men, whom we know as Jan Hudec of Slaný, Martin Křidélko and Stašek Polák, who had been arrested and imprisoned for defending Jan Hus and also for criticizing the indulgences trade four years earlier. Despite protests from Hus and others, including university masters, and assurances from city governmental officials that the detainees would not suffer harm, the three were summarily

---

[73] Jakoubek Stříbro, in FRB, vol. 8, pp. 241-2.

executed on 11 July 1412. Their headless bodies were bravely retrieved, wrapped in white cloths, and then carried in solemn procession from the Old Town Square to the Bethlehem Chapel to the sound of the traditional martyr's antiphon *Isti sunt sancti* (these are saints). An enormous congregation of outraged citizens of Prague formed the great public procession. The following day a martyr's mass was formally sung over them prior to interment in the chapel.[74] Jan Hus said the trio had fallen actively defending truth and he would later be accused of canonizing the new unauthorized Saints Jan, Martin and Stašek.

Hus' journey from Krakovec Castle in Bohemia across assumed hostile German territory to Lake Constance resembled a tour of triumph. There were no efforts to enforce the interdict and in none of the places where he stopped did he encounter animosity as one might expect. People came out to see the heretic and even clerics received him with joy and we have accounts of conversation and meaningful dialogue. One might even say, Hus was something of a celebrity. In the early 1990s, I spent some time at the largely unused regional archives in Tábor in the southern Czech Republic looking at manuscripts and documentary remains from the Hussite period. The archivist was a man named Rudolf Tecl (1950-2005). He received me with great enthusiasm. No sooner had I set to work on some of the materials in the archive than he began calling his friends on his office telephone. I was within earshot. He wanted everyone to know he had a scholar from Cambridge

---

[74] František Šimek and Miloslav Kaňák, eds., *Staré letopisy české z rukopisu křižovnického* (Prague: Státní nakladatelství krásné literatury, hudby a umění, 1959), pp. 4-6.

University in his archive at that very moment, even as he spoke. "Můžete hádat, kdo pracuje v archivu? Ano! On je z Cambridge! CAMBRIDGE! Whoa!!"

Fig. 40: Tábor, Czech Republic

It was extremely annoying. After all, I was trying to concentrate on medieval Latin and Czech texts. But Tecl kept making telephone calls. "CAMBRIDGE! Whoa!!" After some time it became very funny. I would estimate that Archivist Tecl made no fewer than six or eight telephone calls in succession. He was very enthusiastic. At least once (between those repeated and excited telephone announcements) he came to my desk and asked me if I really was from Cambridge, as though he wanted to be quite sure he had the extraordinary story straight. He smiled with deep satisfaction when I confirmed that I had indeed come to Tábor from Cambridge University. He then went and placed several more telephone calls loudly announcing my presence: "CAMBRIDGE! Whoa!!" I had the sense that I was the event of the month in the regional archives at Tábor. I never saw Rudolf

Tecl again after that brief research stint. I was, of course, unaware that despite his loud and excited telephone conversations, Tecl suffered from serious depression. Several years thereafter, on the very eve of his daughter's wedding, the poor man hanged himself from the rafters of the same archive in which he had once announced the presence of a celebrity scholar from Cambridge. The bride-to-be, having gone to search for him, had the dreadful misfortune of being the one to discover her father's body.

Fig. 41: The "Konzil", Constance, Germany

Jan Hus arrived at Constance on 3 November 1414 and found lodgings in the Pfister House in St. Paul Street where the good widow Fida lived.[75] That particular dwelling is now known as *Zur roten Kanne* – "The Red Can" located at the modern city address of Hussenstraße 22. Fida was considered an

---

[75] Thomas Martin Buck, ed., *Chronik des Konstanzer Konzils 1414-1418 von Ulrich Richental* (Ostfildern: Jan Thorbecke Verlag, 2010), p. 60.

"honest and noble widow."[76] The current Jan Hus Museum located at Hussenstraße 64 claims that Hus was accommodated there. He resided in St. Paul Street until 28 November when the house was surrounded suddenly by armed guards and he was arrested and taken into custody. The devoted widow Fida bade him farewell with tears. Following the appearance of my first book on Jan Hus, I was appointed to the University of New England, not in Maine, but in the town of Armidale, in New South Wales, Australia. I had left the antipodes at the end of 2003 assuming my career would continue in the northern hemisphere only to discover that the next chapter in my intellectual and professional journey awaited me back down under. In the past ten years, among other publications, I have written four books on Jan Hus, along with several other book chapters and journal articles. I also recall somewhat ruefully the unsound advice given to me in Prague in 1991 to the effect that Jan Hus as a subject of scholarly inquiry had been completely exhausted. I can also hardly suppress a wry smile when I recall similar unsolicited advice from John "Elephant" Stanley (as Skip Paynter used to call him) at the 1989 Chicago SBL/AAR conference about how I would never get a job if I insisted on going up to Cambridge and working on Jan Hus. His "pillar of fire" wife, Susie Cunningham Stanley, had fervently supported her husband's prophecy and urged me to take seriously

---

[76] František Šimek, ed., *Staré letopisy české z vratislavského rukopisu novočeským pravopisem* (Prague: Historické spolku a společnosti Husova Musea, 1937), p. 13 and Gernot Blechner, "Wo in Konstanz war die Herberge des Jan Hus? - Eine Hauslokalisierung anhand zeitgenössischen Quellenmaterials" *Schriften des Vereins für Geschichte des Bodensees und seiner Umgebung* 101 (1983), pp. 49-71.

that counsel. After all, Dr. Stanley had often intoned in his classrooms the mantra that "repetition equals significance." That was not always true.

My own contributions to the historiography of Hussitica have continued to grow. In terms of Hus, I have now written and published more than 1,700 pages. My work on Hussite history, more broadly speaking, adds to that total another 2,100 pages or more than 3,800 pages in print about Hus and his legacy. My other four books are on unrelated topics. In my first book on Hus, the bibliography of sources fills up an entire twenty-eight printed pages, far exceeding my youthful declaration that there could not possibly be more than forty items. Indeed, my own publications on Hus currently stand at about half that number. I have long surpassed Matthew Spinka's research outputs and have now published

Fig. 42: Cole P. Dawson,
Warner Pacific College, c.2010

more in the English language on Hus and Hussite history than anyone else in history. Doubtlessly, Dr. Cole P. Dawson now has the definite and definitive last laugh. In recommending me to the faculty of Warner Pacific, Bob Scribner apparently told the committee that I would soon emerge as the leading authority on Hussite history.[77] The prediction was generous but I have always been keenly aware of my intellectual debt to Scribner.

Two additional turning points elevated my thinking about Hus and prompted the collation of research into the publications just noted. The first was the commissioning of a book on Hussite history in 2008 which ultimately led to the production of four volumes about Jan Hus. The second event was much more prosaic and occurred at the Center for Christian Studies (CCS) in Portland. I gave a lecture at CCS on 14 October 2009 on the Hus trial. During the general question and answer period, I was asked if I believed that Jan Hus got what he deserved. The query placed me into an uncomfortable position. My lecture had indeed tacitly suggested that very conclusion but when I was confronted with the stark implication of my lecture I was loath to actually admit out loud that the outcome at Constance was proper. I cannot recall with any clarity the nature or import of my reply, but I recall going back to the drawing board with that query in mind intent on solving a troublesome matter. Four years later, my analysis of the Hus trial was published by Oxford University Press. In that particular monograph, which I continue to firmly believe is my most important contribution to the study of Hus, I began my work by attempting to answer a challenging question initially posed by Howard Kaminsky as long ago as 1967. "What the historian wants is not a careful demonstration that Hus should not have

---

[77] "Warner Grad Becomes Religion Scholar," p. 13.

been burned, but a reasonable explanation—in a sense even a justification—of why he was."[78] I went on confidently and declared that my book would satisfy that suggestion.[79] After a more than 150,000 word analysis, I was able to arrive at the conclusion I had already suspected back in 2009. Thus I wrote: "The truth is, by the strict application of medieval law and legal procedure in heresy trials, Jan Hus got what he deserved."[80] A number of my friends and colleagues were displeased.

Following his arrest, Hus was remanded to a prison in the Dominican Monastery built on a small island just offshore. It was a very dark and murky

Fig. 43: Chapter House of the Dominican Monastery, Constance, 14th century

dungeon situated in an unhealthy environment. The miserable situation which Hus was forced to endure in a dank cell near the latrines in the Dominican

---

[78] Howard Kaminsky, *A History of the Hussite Revolution* (Berkeley: University of California Press, 1967), p. 35.
[79] Fudge, *The Trial of Jan Hus*, p. xix.
[80] Fudge, *The Trial of Jan Hus*, p. 340.

monastery lasted nearly five weeks. Meanwhile, a hitherto unnoticed source makes a single mention of the fact that Pope John XXIII paid for repairs in the Dominican dungeon, which included the installation of a chimney and six beds for guards appointed to keep Hus secure. Payments were then made on a monthly basis between December and April to this very end. The chimney provided heat for the guards. This was most extraordinary. Twelve guards for one man on an island! The repairs imply making the dungeon space secure for the incarceration of an offender.[81] Above the main entrance to the chapter house, one can still make out the date 1339 carved in stone.

I spent a good part of the winter of 1991-92 in Prague. I was frequently invited to join my friends Blanka Šmídlová and Olga Váchova for dinner and an evening at Olga's house, never at Blanka's, at 24 Kubelíkova Street in the Žižkov district. On these occasions I was regaled with sometimes colorful stories and anecdotal insights into Czech history as well as an understanding of Hus' role in Czech history from the standpoint of popular imagination. David Holeton had been expected to come from Canada but he fell ill. In due course it became clear he would not be travelling to Prague any time soon

---

[81] Prato Biblioteca Roncioniana, Manoscritti, R. VIII.43 (336), pp. 63 and 64. The information for the repair of the dungeon is from December 1414 and for building the chimney is from January 1415. I am grateful to Henry Gerlach for the reference which was more fully articulated in Henry Gerlach, "Papst Johannes XXIII. und Jan Hus – Neue Erkenntnisse zu einer alten Feindschaft," a paper which Gerlach presented at "The VII International Hussitological Symposium Jan Hus 1415 and 600 Years After" in Tábor, Czech Republic, 23 June 2015. It was normal for two soldiers to sleep in one bed.

for his restorative pig blood soup. This fact did not prevent Olga, one winter evening, from asking the repeated question over and over, "vhen vill David come?" She then proceeded to answer her own question with the mournful refrain, "I don't know, I don't know" all the while wringing her hands as though distraught over an unspoken impending catastrophe. Once Jan Hus had disappeared into dungeons hired by Council officials, many of his friends in Prague must surely have asked the same question as Olga did: when will Master Hus return? Of course he was not to see his homeland again.

More generally, my understanding of Hus has, after thirty years of research, arrived at several firm conclusions. He is best understood, I believe, as a Catholic reformer rather than a rebel desiring to initiate a new movement. His trial was regrettable, even though it was legal, and the outcome cannot be reasonably characterized either as judicial murder or legal malfeasance. That said, not everything which is permitted, or legal, is honest or right.[82] My work has irredeemably eroded my previous assumption that Hus was a forerunner of Luther and I am now firmly convinced that the broad thrust of Protestant and reformation historiography is just not a reliable guide when exploring the medieval Hussite world. On account of Scribner's influence, I have looked extensively into the historical evidence embedded in visual culture and in the surviving texts of songs and have paid close attention to the presence of Hus in art and in music and have published on both topics. It is also possible to make the argument that Hus was unprepared to retreat from his position on important matters like truth and reform. Whatever

---

[82] "*Non omne quod licet honestum est.*" D 50.17.144 (Paulus).

did not agree with apostolic teaching and the law of God, Hus refused to consider and went so far as to declare "I will not obey, even if the fire to destroy my body is placed in front of me."[83]

The Constance Cathedral is an historic building which has undergone architectural modifications over a period of several hundred years. The only pope ever elected to the papacy north of the Alps occurred here in Constance and Pope Martin V was enthroned in the cathedral in 1417. He had been involved in the Jan Hus case for several years. A wooden pulpit support was defaced and spat upon, in the centuries after Hus was condemned within the cathedral, by many common people who mistakenly thought the support featured Hus the heretic who was made to atone for his sin by carrying the sacred desk from whence all truth was proclaimed. The cathedral also features another curiosity. Near the rear of the nave, in the center aisle, one can see a stain on the floor. This is traditionally thought to be the very spot where Hus stood when he heard the sentence of death pronounced. From that time on, the spot darkened and could never be repaired. Was it the hand of Satan, or an expression of divine disfavor? Both explanations have had many fervent defenders over the years.

Like Jan Hus, I have spent a lifetime associated with the church in one fashion or another. I allowed myself to be persuaded to consider the priesthood in the Episcopal Church and even went through the preliminary process but, unlike Hus, I was never under holy orders. I have every sense that Hus was a passionate preacher delivering energetic sermons

---

[83] *Contra octo doctores*, in MIHO, vol. 22, pp. 475-6.

which had clear relevance for his hearers. History is not boring, although many of its teachers are. The gospel is also not boring and the announcement of

Fig. 44: Preaching at St. Anne's Episcopal Church, Washougal, WA, September 2012

the good news should convey the same energy and passion that accompanied its initial communication. Living with Jan Hus has reinforced that principle. I learned from Hus that while right and wrong may not have any meaning whatsoever, truth does. His emphasis on moral reform applied to everyone and not even the higher clergy and prelates of the church were exempt. During the time of my youth, I recall the "organization" was virtually untouchable. The preachers ruled with an unyielding iron fist and a stentorian King James Version voice of authority. All challenges to their ecclesiastical fiefdom were answered with a text taken well out of context from the Hebrew Bible: "touch not mine anointed."[84] Hus

---

[84] Psalm 105:15 and I Chronicles 16:22.

went against the grain and touched them with some force even denouncing his wayward colleagues as "egotistical, parasites, bulls in heat, merchants of greed, fat pigs, spiritual fornicators, greedy wolves, drunkards, and gluttons whose stomachs are so engorged, their double chins hang down."[85]

While incarcerated in three different prisons in the city of Constance, Hus wrote numerous letters to various addressees. We possess about fifty of these surviving letters. His valuable correspondence reveal unguarded, private thoughts wherein we find meditations which reflect his deep humanity, hopes, fears, dreams (real and those nocturnally-induced), mood, emotions, and so on. While in prison, Hus had time to think. He had opportunity for reflection. We read accounts of letters hidden under meal trays being smuggled in and out of Hus' prison cell.[86] The words he wrote down, sometimes on little more than tiny scraps of paper, are surely the considered thoughts of a human mind revealing elements of passion and personality. We must be ever grateful to those anonymous prison guards who breached protocol and facilitated our understanding of these dark and otherwise unknown days in the life of Hus. We can only wonder about those thoughts which either he never recorded or which have been lost to history. How did he view his life? Did Jan Hus fear death? Did he ever feel like a failure? Medieval men and women did not often bequeath to history intimate revelations.

---

[85] These are extracts from Hus' sermons in Flajšhans, ed., *Mag. Io. Hus Sermones in Capella Bethlehem, 1410-1411*, and summarized succinctly in Fudge, *The Memory and Motivation of Jan Hus, Medieval Priest and Martyr*, pp. 81-2.
[86] Vavřinec of Březová, *Historia Hussitica* in FRB, vol 5, pp. 332-3.

On a warm summer evening in 1994, David Holeton and I, along with one of David's students from Toronto named Charles Wallace, went up on the Žižkov in Prague after dark. I remember that student's name all these years later because he had the same name as my maternal grandfather: Charles Wallace. The Žižkov is a hill prominent in Czech history. It lies just to the east of the Old Town. Here in July 1420, Jan Žižka won the battle of the first crusade over the invading imperial armies. One of the largest equestrian statutes in the world, featuring Žižka, stands on top of the Žižkov. As the three of us stood looking down on the lights of Prague, I became aware that Holeton had fallen into silence. After we returned to Olga Váchova's house, where the three of us were staying, I asked David if he was all right. I remember vividly his reply when he said that sometimes it was rather depressing going up there at night. It was like looking out over the world and reflecting on a wasted life. I never forgot those words. They reminded me of the sage and solemn insight once spoken by Henry David Thoreau of the greatest tragedy of coming to life's end only to discover one had not lived. Did Hus ever think of his life as wasted? He never said so. However, we do find in one letter a resolve wherein he expressed that "it is better to die well than to live badly."[87]

I recall working in the Prague Castle Archive in the summer of 1991. Day after day and week after long week, I was the only researcher working with medieval manuscripts belonging to the historic Cathedral Chapter Library. In those days, now long gone, the director of the Prague Castle archives was Marie Kostílková. She facilitated my solitary work

---

[87] Novotný, *Correspondence*, pp. 169-70.

with kindness and competence. Her English was very poor and my Czech even poorer but her smile was warm and winning and I remember the many

Fig. 45: Prague Castle

treasures she carried to my desk during those long days in the castle. Marie died in 2004 at the age of seventy. Just as Hus' jailors allowed him to stay in regular contact with the outside world, so Marie's willingness to endure my constant interruptions of her own work allowed me to get closer to my goal of finding the historical Hus.

I learned from Jan Hus more perfect dimensions of pastoral care. One example and a contemporary testimony must suffice. In the spring of 1403 the episcopal warrior Zbyněk was commissioned by Václav IV, king of Bohemia, to bring to justice a robber bandit named Jan Zúl of Ostředek. In time, the archbishop captured the fugitive who was then sentenced to be hanged along with his men. At the gallows Hus accompanied the condemned man to his public execution and succeeded in bringing the criminal to repentance. A contemporary chronicle records Zúl asking the people gathered to pray to

God for his soul.[88] This minor incident shows Hus the pastor actively engaged in the work of ministry, taking time for even the most unworthy. A few

Fig. 46: Jan Hus at Worms, Germany.
Detail of the Luther monument

years later Hus set down a brief exposition of the duties of a priest. He included five in number: preaching the gospel, prayer, the ministry of the sacraments, study of the scriptures, and setting the example of good works.[89] His own career admirably

---

[88] Šimek, ed., *Staré letopisy české z vratislavského rukopisu novočeským pravopisem*, p. 5.

[89] *De quinque officiis sacerdotis*, in Anon., [Matthias Flacius Illyricus], ed. *Historia et monumenta Ioannis Hus atque Hieronymi Pragensis*, 2 vols (Nürnberg: Montanus and Neuberus, 1558; 1715), vol. 1, p. 191.

reflected all five. Dated 23 May 1416, the venerable Charles University in Prague provided testimony about Jan Hus.

> O incomparable man shining greater than all by the example of magnificent holiness. O humble man gleaming with the light of great piety, who scorned wealth and ministered to those in poverty. He opened his heart and did not refuse to kneel at the bedside of the sick. With tears he drew the hardened to repentance. By his matchless sweetness he calmed fierce minds. He raged against the vices of humankind particularly the rich and arrogant clergy. He founded his appeals on the ancient and neglected scriptural remedies. Formed in great love, this new motive caused him to follow in the footsteps of the apostles and through pastoral care he revived in both clergy and laity the righteousness of life as in the primitive church. Through courage and wisdom in speech he surpassed all others, demonstrating in all things the works of love, pure faith, and consistent truth. ... in everything he became a master of life without compare.[90]

My pastor, and the man who baptized me at age eleven, was charismatic and dynamic. He was also brutish, uneducated, frequently rude, uncouth, and arrogant. In retrospect, he seemed to me the utter antithesis of Jan Hus. For years, I had heard him preach sermons in which he appealed to the young people of the congregation to take advantage of his willingness to talk and I heard him often say he wanted everyone to have confidence in him. I took up that repeated invitation only once. He told me rather brusquely he did not have the time to speak with me. He provided no indication when we might be able to do so. I was both embarrassed and angry. As part of my application for admission to CBC at age eighteen, I was required to submit my pastor's

---

[90] *Historia et monumenta*, vol. 1, p. 103.

recommendation. His terse comments included a suggestive observation which in retrospect was not inaccurate. "He [TAF] has a mind of his own at times which perhaps might lean toward a bit of rebellion."[91] The form was dated 3 February 1981. I did not see it until August 2013 when I obtained a copy of my student file from the archives of "the organization" when I was working there conducting research. The pastoral comment was correct and my restless, rebellious, spirit has yet to be tempered. I never detected a real evidence of pastoral care, nor did I sense very much beyond basic fear-mongering and manipulation, in my pastor. I gleaned quite the opposite from Jan Hus. More than twenty years after I left the house of heresy for CBC, I heard that my old pastor actually apologized from the pulpit for mistakes he had made in his earlier ministry. I never held any ill-will and I was prepared to accept that expression of regret. There is no life without regret and even Hus must have had his own.

During the night of 24 March 1415, Hus was transferred about two-and-a-half miles west of the city along the Rhine River, under the supervision of Otto von Hachberg, Bishop of Constance, in chains and under the armed escort of 170 men, in a boat.[92] The castle of Gottlieben had been built in 1251. Jan Hus was held in the upper portion of the west tower manacled during the day with one hand chained to the wall at night. I took the same journey by boat three years ago in the brightness of a warm, sunny,

---

[91] CBC, "Pastor's Recommendation" form, p. 3.

[92] *Documenta*, pp. 541-3 and Hermann von der Hardt, ed., *Magnum oecumenicum constantiense concilium*, 7 vols (Frankfurt and Leipzig: C. Genschii, Helmestadi, 1699-1742), vol. 4, p. 66.

summer afternoon in the company of the loveliest of friends. I wondered what Hus thought as he moved slowly down the river under the cover of night so long ago with no friends and no consolation.

Fig. 47: Gottlieben Fortress

As the years passed I have become more keenly aware of two principles evident within the life and career of John G. Diefenbaker who was mentioned earlier. The first has been articulated already and has to do with going against the grain. It would be facile to mount an argument against the attraction I feel to this perspective. The other is a statement Diefenbaker made in 1967 when he stood for party leadership once more, at the last moment, in the face of an upcoming general election, even though he knew he had no chance for success. When asked why he, as a former prime minister, would risk exposing himself to public humiliation, Diefenbaker said: "the probability of defeat is no justification for surrender to a false principle."[93] Diefenbaker made his point. He was defeated.

Lipany is a very small village about twenty-five miles east of Prague. Fewer than 100 people live there today. Almost six centuries ago, a ferocious

Fig. 48: Prokop Holý monument, Český Brod, Czech Republic, 1910, by Karel Opatrný

battle fought on 30 May 1434, not far from the town, virtually annihilated Hussite military power. A stark monument marks the place of that decisive confrontation. On the long wide field, thousands of men were butchered in a carnage that lasted through the night. Up to as many as 13,000 men may have perished. When the realization of the magnitude of the disaster began to dawn upon the warriors, the priest and chief commander of the Hussite armies, Prokop Holý, advised some of his men to run for their lives. Prokop declined to exercise that option

[93] Diefenbaker, *One Canada*, vol. 3: *The Tumultuous Years 1962-1967*, p. 282.

himself and died, sword in hand, for the "faith." As many as another one thousand Hussites were herded into nearby barns and burned alive.[94] Standing there on that awful field of battle, bloodshed and carnage, I had doubts that Hus would have approved of any of it. War is violent and cannot be refined.

I have made little effort to avoid controversy in my work. Like Scribner, I have taken little note of naysayers. Fisher could not be bullied. C.H. Yadon refused to yield to external pressure. Dawson taught us to consistently follow the evidence. Brendlinger insisted on standards and integrity. Luther chalked his position on a table and withstood all detractors. Hus taught me the courage of conviction, absolute devotion to the faith, a refusal to recant for anything other than "truth" and principle, and an unshakeable firm allegiance to truth. These are lessons I would neither dare to say I have learned completely, nor examples I have succeeded in practicing with any consistency. My inheritance from the household of heresy absolved me from all fear of straying outside the boundaries of historiographical orthodoxy or timidity from transgressing established patterns of scholarship. During the post-Communist but chaotic decade of the 1990s, Cardinal Miloslav Vlk, who was also archbishop of Prague, convened what was then called "the commission for the study of the problems connected to the person, life and work of Master Jan Hus." The twenty-six members of this commission met regularly over an eight-and-a-half year period with the specific brief to investigate the

---

[94] Frederick G. Heymann, *John Žižka and the Hussite Revolution* (New York: Russell & Russell, 1969), pp. 468-9 and Fudge, *The Magnificent Ride: The First Reformation in Hussite Bohemia*, p. 115.

details of the life and work of Jan Hus. Anchored within the Czech Catholic Bishops Conference, this unique commission labored to facilitate dialogue between the Czech bishops and the Vatican in view of Pope John Paul II's terse remarks about Jan Hus delivered in Prague Castle on 21 April 1990 to a rapt audience.[95] There was considerable widespread enthusiasm for a papal rehabilitation of Hus. This context represented my first open conflict with other scholars. I opposed the rehabilitation initiative in print in North America and had an exchange with Pope John Paul II on the matter.[96] My efforts to publish my views in Prague were rebuffed but this did not prevent me from publishing on the matter much later.[97] I felt no obligation to support church expressions of political correctness and no loyalty to ecumenical initiatives which, in my considered view, sought to manipulate and control history. Jan Hus would have agreed. His life is the evidence.

After months of wrangling, Jan Hus was finally granted a series of public hearings. They were held in what was formerly the Franciscan monastery in Constance. The manacled heretic faced the power and authority of the Latin Church in the monastery refectory. The Franciscans disappeared long ago. Today the site is occupied by a school and where the refectory may have been, there is now a hall used by various civic organizations for recitals and exhibitions. There is no trace of Hus.

---

[95] Quoted in Fudge, *Jan Hus: Religious Reform and Social Revolution in Bohemia*, p. 229.

[96] Thomas A. Fudge, "Infoelix Hus": The Rehabilitation of a Medieval Heretic" *Fides et Historia* 30 (No. 1, 1998), pp. 57-73.

[97] Fudge, *Jan Hus: Religious Reform and Social Revolution in Bohemia*, pp. 227-40.

My second conflict was over language. I have steadfastly refused to yield to the argument that the term "Hussite" is inappropriate for describing Hus' followers and I have even more stridently insisted upon referring to Hus as a heretic. Several of my publications refer to Hus as a heretic in the title. I do not regard the nomenclature either as negative or prejudicial. This doubtlessly is a direct product of my religious upbringing. Heresy accusations rarely relate to faith or theology specifically. Instead, they have more to do with considerations of power and control. In other words, issues of faith, theological perspectives, or religious practice are used as the means for advancing heresy charges. In a religious context, an adversary is sometimes denounced as a heretic while different points of view are labelled heresy. The nomenclature is appropriate and useful for distinguishing boundaries and for determining identity. It serves to indicate how groups perceive threats or compromises in relation to their basic and essential values.[98] There is nothing abnormal or necessarily negative about determining "heretics" and "heresies." In the most cogent of definitions, a heretic is an individual who challenges a closed system of presumed or declared truth.[99] It does not make them bad, dangerous, or evil.

A story of dubious historicity, which has been preserved from the fifteenth century, reveals that during one cold winter night Jan Hus got out of his

---

[98] A very brief but useful discussion appears in Thomas A. Robinson, "Doing Double Duty: David Reed as Apologist and Critic of Oneness Pentecostalism" *Canadian Journal of Pentecostal-Charismatic Christianity* 1 (2010), pp. 86-87.

[99] There is a helpful overview in George H. Shriver, ed., *American Religious Heretics: Formal and Informal Trials* (Nashville: Abingdon Press, 1966), pp. 13-17.

bed and kindled a fire in the stove. Kneeling before
the heat he prayed. While in fervent devotion, he
took a hot glowing piece of wood and held it to his

FOR YHOMAS   S.L   2010 PRAHA

Fig. 49: Stephen E. Lahey, Hus with the
glowing coal, 2010. Pencil drawing

exposed flesh. Having burned himself, he quickly
threw the ember back into the flames unable to
endure the pain. He then confessed his weakness
saying, "Oh Lord God, you know my weakness and
you can see how faint-hearted I am when suffering,
because I am human, and unless you help me, I will
not be able to overcome and do your holy work."
All of this drama was apparently witnessed by
another man who had also arisen to light the fire to
warm the house. Peering into the fire, this second
man saw, what he took to be, an angel standing in
the flames. Much later, this man told Hus what he

had seen that winter night. Hus begged this man not to tell anyone, warning him that should he disclose any details of the incident he would soon die. So the anonymous witness, fearing for his own life, did not speak of the incident until many years after the death of Jan Hus.[100] The first time I spoke publicly about this strange, nocturnal, incident, was during a conference in Prague, and one of my colleagues in the audience sketched his concept of Hus' early martyrological consciousness in conjunction with my lecture description.[101]

Hus was incarcerated for 219 days, just over seven months. The final events in his trial occurred on 6 July in the cathedral at Constance. Those final acts commenced at 6:00 a.m. Session fifteen was presided over by the Cardinal-Priest John Brogli of Ostia. Odo Colonna, the future Pope Martin V, was there.[102] Mass was celebrated by the Pole Mikołaj Trąba, Archbishop of Gniezno. Hus and his escort, Johann Wallenrode, the archbishop of Riga, had to wait outside closed doors until the celebration of the eucharist had been concluded.[103] There are three principle doors to the cathedral. The main entrance, in 1415, opened directly onto the main road running through the city. It is doubtful the Council wished for Hus to be left there. The north entrance opened

---

[100] "The Life of Jan Hus by George the Hermit," in FRB, vol. 8, p. 378.

[101] The drawing was made by Stephen E. Lahey, Happold Professor of Religious Studies at the University of Nebraska, in Lincoln and was presented to me following the lecture. It is dated 2010.

[102] Czech *Acta* in the Freiburg Codex, in FRB, vol. 8, p. 260.

[103] *Passio of Master Jan Hus*, in FRB, vol. 8, p. 127 and Dietrich Niem, *De vita ac fatis Constantiensibus Johannis Papae XXIII* in Hardt, vol. 2, col. 408.

into a public marketplace. This would have been
another busy area. But the south entrance led into a
closed courtyard immediately before the residence

Fig. 50: Cathedral of Constance

of the bishop. It is likely that here the condemned
man waited to hear the verdict. It is possible he
could hear the ringing of bells at the altar and may
have listened to the distant liturgical chants and the
swelling singing of the congregation. Beyond the
closed door of the church was just as close as an
excommunicate could come. Jan Hus had already
been subjected to bell, book, and candle.

Thirty years of research have convinced me that
by the prevailing standards and definitions of the
later Middle Ages, Hus was a heretic. This was my
third controversy. For this unpopular view, I have
been criticized by colleagues and labelled by others
as a right wing Roman Catholic. I have always felt
an attraction to the heretics and dissenters, to those

who resisted the tyranny of the majority, those who always deliberately went against the grain, those who consistently attempted to practice intellectual honesty, and those who viewed nonconformity, not as a vice but, as a virtue. Regulated thinking had to be stoutly resisted. Thus in 1412, Hus rejected the insistence of King Václav IV who wanted to impose some control over the university. Hus facetiously suggested that the king was arguing that it would be good for the city of Prague, for the university itself, as well as all the masters and scholars if offenders, which included any master, student, or even the lord rector, were detained and locked up, if they refused to obey. Hus went on to suggest that if the king wished to enforce his will, he should just establish an academic prison.[104] Martin Luther, Bob Scribner, Donald Fisher, C.H. Yadon, and of course Jan Hus himself, were all definite heretics. The fellowship of that fraternity has been stimulating and sustaining.

The simple Romanesque three-aisled cathedral in Constance was greatly modified for the Council proceedings. Seats had been constructed. The high altar covered. Another altar had been built as well as several thrones. The nave had been walled in along the columns. Within the nave, extending the full length were three rows of seats facing each other. On the highest sat the cardinals, archbishops and princes. On the second level were the bishops and abbots. On the first level were the proctors, notaries and theologians. Moveable seats were set up at floor level and these were filled mainly with priests and lawyers. In the midst of the nave a pulpit

---

[104] *Documenta*, pp. 450-1.

had been set up.[105] It is from this place, where Hus
walked to his death, a foot journey which may have
required fifteen minutes. I have often stood in the
precincts of this church, in the dimness and in the
silence, and tried to imagine what it must have been
like on that Saturday morning, 600 years ago.

Erected in 1862, the so-called Hussenstein is the
traditional place where Master Jan Hus reached the
intersection of time and eternity and crossed the bar.

Fig. 51: The Hussenstein, Constance

From the ashes of the stake, the historical Hus was
transformed into an icon which over time has served
many purposes ranging from political to religious.
Politicizing the legend of Jan Hus has quite serious
dimensions for scholarship and in some quarters
Hus continues to be held hostage by certain special
interests groups. In June 2015 I gave a controversial

---

[105] Richental, *Chronik*, in Buck, pp. 18-19 and Heribert
Reiners, *Das Münster unserer lieben Frau zu Konstanz*
(Constance: Thorbecke, 1955), pp. 12-20, 46-7.

lecture at an international conference convened in the Czech Republic. I assailed the formation and perpetuation of the Jan Hus legend and called for scholars to actively resist. Implicitly, I argued that my critique of particular structures, institutions, and attitudes was neither antithetical to the duty of the historian nor inconsistent with the approach of Jan Hus himself. This particular lecture and point of view constitutes my fourth controversy as a Hus scholar. In late years I have discovered that I am no more amendable to the "message" about Jan Hus or to the "organization" which promotes it any more

Fig. 52: Stephen E. Lahey, "The Grand Rabbinic Council," 2015. Water color

than I was content to bask in the baleful climate of that other "organization" more than half a lifetime ago. Several colleagues, aware in advance of the general thrust of my lecture, purchased an eye patch for me reminiscent of the one-eyed, and then later completely blind, Hussite military commander Jan Žižka. This was a joke about the fact that my talk might incite the audience of mainly Czech scholars to rise up and put out one of my eyes.[106] Three days after the conference presentation (which angered at least a few of the delegates), one of my colleagues executed an amusing and very telling water-color representation of the Czech academy which very deliberately and quite firmly made clear that I was not, and never would be, a member.[107]

While I am keenly interested in the findings and arguments of other scholars, I feel no obligation to adjust my research to theirs or to defer my own conclusions to theirs, regardless of how astute or subtle those arguments may be. I do not accept the notion of a mainstream or consensus approach to understanding Jan Hus. The idea of a mainstream is only a construct created, sustained, and recognized by scholars much like historic periodization. It may be convenient but remains artificial. The notion of a mainstream interpretation of Hus is not helpful and I refuse to recognize it.[108] Presumably, the idea of a mainstream understanding of Hus corresponds in some sense to the work of certain Czech scholars including luminaries such as František Palacký, Václav Novotný, Vlastimil Kybal, and František M. Bartoš, or the Belgian Benedictine Paul de Vooght, or the Czech-American academic Matthew Spinka.

---

[106] The eye patch was bought at the Hussite Museum in Tábor by Trish Wright, the Academic Coordinator for the School of Humanities, at the University of New England in Australia, Professor Stephen Lahey, University of Nebraska in Lincoln, Professor Jeanne Grant, Metropolitan State University, in St. Paul, Minnesota, and Henry Gerlach, a local historian from Constance, Germany.

[107] The art work was prepared by the aforementioned Stephen Lahey who once more presented the finished product to me during an excursion to Karlštejn Castle.

[108] Fudge, *Jan Hus: Religious Reform and Social Revolution in Bohemia*, p. 4.

These are the holy names in Jan Hus historiography. I have learned much from their erudite work but I disagree with them all in many ways. My refusal to acquiesce in consensus views or participate in the mainstream of historiographical perspective has been noted by some colleagues with puzzlement or even disdain. A recent review of one of my books included comments which are fairly representative. "Fudge positions himself outside the mainstream of scholarly writings on Hus and the case against him." That is a cogent observation which cannot be gainsaid. The same writer went on to remark that it was "unfortunate that his volume does not engage more with the scholarly mainstream."[109] Such comments might easily be multiplied. But what is the mainstream? How is that defined and by whom? Why is it unfortunate that my work fails to engage with this mainstream? However these queries are answered by others, I think my general aversion to consensus scholarship is linked with my firm and innate commitment to the Diefenbaker doctrine.

Epilogue

This opportunity to remember, recognize, and reflect, takes me back along many roads of the past where the faces of all my travelling companions appear once more through the mists of time and memory. Among a host of others, these include Bob Scribner, Martin Luther, Roland Bainton, Jiří Kejř, Don Fisher, C.H. Yadon, David Holeton, my father, Irv Brendlinger, Cole Dawson, Rod Colbin, Libor Brom, John Diefenbaker, Merydith Mitts, Matthew

---

[109] J. Patrick Hornbeck II in a review of *The Trial of Jan Hus* in *Church History* 83 (No. 3, 2014), pp. 750-2.

Spinka, each of the "inepters", the "cat in the hat", Franz Bibfeldt, and of course, Jan Hus himself. I have neither forgotten any of these nor regretted the journey. From Canada to the antipodes, CBC to Cambridge, from Warner Pacific College (WPC) to Canterbury University, from Iliff to the Northern Tablelands of New South Wales and UNE, and with more than two dozen trips to Prague scattered in between, this fulfilling modern, personal, journey across a fascinating medieval landscape continues. Of course, I cannot possibly know how many chapters remain in the book of my life, for the last ones have yet to be written.

On 6 October 1904, the *New York Times* ran a small section headline with a stark announcement: "Dr. Samuel F. Upham dead." One day earlier, the well-known and respected Dr. Samuel Foster Upham, who had been the Professor of Practical Theology at Drew Theological Seminary in New Jersey, lay dying. Friends and family had gathered around the bed and at length the question arose if Upham was still alive. At length, someone shrewdly advanced the suggestion, "feel his feet. No one ever died with warm feet." At that precise moment, Dr. Upham opened one eye and drily said, "Jan Hus did." Those were his last words. [110]

Jan Hus has been dead more than 600 years. I have lived in the shadow of his life for more than thirty years. I have come to understand him as a medieval Catholic reformer, hobbled by naïveté, cultivating a martyr-complex, and so truculent in his own views as to be immune to reason. I have not discovered any compelling evidence which forces

---

[110] Editorial, *The Christian Century* 71 (7 July, 1954), p. 817.

me to characterize him as a true front-rank thinker. Regardless of the different masks he has been made to wear over the centuries, Hus remains for me a

Fig. 53: Hus memorial at Tábor, 1928, by František Bílek

reforming priest, committed unswervingly to truth as he understood it. Hus was a man of conscience, completely devoted to principle, whose life was defined mainly by the manner of his death. As noted above, Poggio Bracciolini was not a witness to Hus' death and he did not compose any account of it. However, he did write a stirring letter about the burning of Jerome of Prague the following year. Poggio firmly insisted that Jerome "was a man to remember."[111] If I first glimpsed Jan Hus in the

---

[111] Poggio Bracciolini, letter to Leonardo Bruni, 30 May 1416 appears in a critical edition in Helene Harth, ed., *Poggio*

features of Rod Colbin in 1981, I now see him as a fifteenth-century man in pursuit of truth.

Standing in the former Brüel Field outside the old medieval city walls of Constance, under a blazing summer sun or beneath winter snow flakes looking at the Hussenstein, marking the place where Master Jan Hus finally surrendered to the silence of eternity, I have realized that the medieval landscape still has the power to impress and persuade those of us who remain on pilgrimage through a turbulent modern world. I have intentionally chosen to devote part of my professional life to this fascinating man because I agree with Poggio and that across the years one spirit may indeed kindle another and I have warmed my hands before the fire of Jan Hus' life.[112]

Bracciolini Lettere, 3 vols (Florence: Leo S. Olschki, 1984-7), vol. 2 *Epistolarum familiarium libri*, pp. 157-63.

[112] I borrow the analogy from Roland H. Bainton, *Studies on the Reformation* (London: Hodder and Stoughton, 1963), p. 184.

Select Bibliography of Scholarship in English

Primary Sources

Fudge, Thomas A. "Jan Hus at 'Calvary': The Text of an Early Fifteenth-Century Passio." *Journal of Moravian History* 11 (Fall, 2011), pp. 45-81.

Holeton, David R. "The Office of Jan Hus: An Unrecorded Antiphonary in the Metropolitical Library of Estergom." In J. Neil Alexander, ed. *Time and Community* [Festschrift for Thomas J. Talley]. Washington DC: The Pastoral Press, 1990, pp. 137-152.

Schaff, David S., trans. *The Church by John Huss*. New York: Scribner's, 1915.

Spinka, Matthew, ed. *Advocates of Reform*. Philadelphia: Westminster Press, 1953.

_____. *John Hus at the Council of Constance*. New York: Columbia University Press, 1965.

_____, trans. *The Letters of John Hus*. Manchester: Manchester University Press, 1972.

Secondary Sources

Crews, C. Daniel. "The Theology of John Hus with Special Reference to His Concepts of Salvation." PhD dissertation, University of Manchester, 1975.

Didomizio, Daniel. "Jan Hus's *De ecclesia*, Precursor of Vatican II?" *Theological Studies* 60 (No. 2, 1999), pp. 247-260.

Fudge, Thomas A. "'Ansellus dei' and the Bethlehem Chapel in Prague." *Communio viatorum* 35 (No. 2, 1993), pp. 127-161.

Fudge, Thomas A. "Art and Propaganda in Hussite Bohemia." *Religio: Revue pro religionistiku* 2 (No. 1, 1993), pp. 135-153.

_____. "The State of Hussite Historiography." *Mediaevistik: Internationale Zeitschrift für interdisziplinäre Mittelalterforschung* 7 (1994), pp. 93-117.

_____. "'The Shouting Hus:' Heresy Appropriated as Propaganda in the Sixteenth Century." *Communio viatorum* 38 (No. 3, 1996), pp. 197-231.

_____. *The Magnificent Ride: The First Reformation in Hussite Bohemia.* Aldershot: Ashgate, 1998.

_____. "'Infoelix Hus:' The Rehabilitation of a Medieval Heretic." *Fides et Historia* 30 (No. 1, 1998), pp. 57-73.

_____. "Hussite Theology and the Law of God." In David Bagchi and David C. Steinmetz, eds. *The Cambridge Companion to Reformation Theology.* Cambridge: Cambridge University Press, 2004, pp. 22-27.

_____. "Picturing the Death and Life of Jan Hus in the Iconography of Early Modern Europe." *Kosmas: Czechoslovak and Central European Journal* 23 (No. 1, 2009), pp. 1-18.

_____. *Heresy and Hussites in Late Medieval Europe.* Aldershot: Ashgate, 2014.

_____. *The Trial of Jan Hus: Medieval Heresy and Criminal Procedure.* New York: Oxford University Press, 2013.

_____. *The Memory and Motivation of Jan Hus, Medieval Priest and Martyr.* Turnhout: Brepols, 2013.

Fudge, Thomas A. *Jan Hus: Religious Reform and Social Revolution in Bohemia.* London and New York: I.B. Tauris Publishers, 2010.

_____. "Jan Hus in the Medieval Ecclesiastical Courts." In *Political Trials: Interdisciplinary Perspectives.* Eds. Jens Meierhenrich and Devin O. Pendas. Cambridge: Cambridge University Press, in press.

_____. "O Cursed Judas: Formal Heresy Accusations against Jan Hus." In *Religion, Power and Resistance from the Eleventh to the Sixteenth Centuries: Playing the Heresy Card.* Eds, Thomas M. Izbicki, Karen Bollermann, and Cary J. Nederman. New York: Palgrave-Macmillan, 2014, pp. 55-80.

_____. "Jan Hus as the Apocalyptic Witness in John Foxe's History." *Communio Viatorum* 56 (No.2, 2014): 136-168.

_____. *Jan Hus Between Time and Eternity: Reconsidering a Medieval Heretic.* Lanham, MD: Lexington Books, 2016.

_____. "Jan Hus in English Language Historiography, 1863-2013." *Journal of Moravian History*, forthcoming.

Gaybba, B. "John Huss' views on the nature of theology in the introduction to his commentary on the Sentences." *Studia historiae ecclesiasticae* 20 (No. 2, 1994), pp. 79-94.

Haberkern, Phillip. "'After Me There Will Come Braver Men:' Jan Hus and Reformation Polemics in the 1530s." *German History* 27 (No. 2, 2009), pp. 177-195.

Haberkern, Phillip. *Patron Saint and Prophet: Jan Hus in the Bohemian and German Reformation* (New York: Oxford University Press, 2016).

_____. "What's in a Name, or What's at Stake When we Talk about 'Hussites'?" *History Compass* 9 (No. 10, 2011), pp. 791-801.

Herold, Vilém. "Jan Hus - A Heretic, a Saint, or a Reformer?" *Kosmas: Czechoslovak and Central European Journal* 15 (No. 1, 2001), pp. 1-15.

Holeček, František J. "The Problems of the Person, the Life and the Work of Jan Hus: The Significance and the Task of a Commission of the Czech Bishops' Conference." *The Bohemian Reformation and Religious Practice* 2 (1998), pp. 39-47.

Holeton, David R. "'O felix Bohemia - O felix Constantia:' The Liturgical Celebration of Saint Jan Hus." In Ferdinand Seibt, ed. *Jan Hus: Zwischen Zeiten, Völkern, Konfessionen.* Munich: Oldenbourg, 1997, pp. 385-403.

_____. "The Celebration of Jan Hus in the Life of the Churches." *Studia Liturgica* 35 (2005), pp. 32-59.

_____ and Hana Vlhová-Wörner. "A Remarkable Witness to the Feast of Saint Jan Hus." *The Bohemian Reformation and Religious Practice* 7 (2009), pp. 156-84.

Klassen, John M. "Hus, the Hussites and Bohemia." In Christopher Allmand, ed. *The New Cambridge Medieval History*, vol. 7, Cambridge, Cambridge University Press, 1998, pp. 367-391.

Kubíková, Milena. "The Heretic's Cap of Hus." *The Bohemian Reformation and Religious Practice* 4 (2002), pp. 143-150.

Leff, Gordon. "Wyclif and Hus: A Doctrinal Comparison." *Bulletin of the John Rylands Library* 50 (1967-8), pp. 387-410.

Lützow, Count [František]. *The Life and Times of Master John Hus.* London: Dent, 1909.

Matula, Jozef. "The Understanding of Time and Eternity in the Philosophy of Magister John Hus." In Gerhard Jaritz and Gerson Moreno-Riaño, eds. *Time and Eternity: The Medieval Discourse.* Turnhout: Brepols, 2003, pp. 223-30.

Molnar, Enrico. "The liturgical reforms of John Hus." *Speculum* 41 (April 1966), pp. 297-303.

Morée, Peter, C.A. "Jan Hus as a Threat to the German Future in Central Europe: The Bohemian Reformer in the Controversy Between Constantin Höfler and František Palacký." *The Bohemian Reformation and Religious Practice* 4 (2002), pp. 295-307.

_____. "Not Preaching from the Pulpit, but Marching in the Streets: The Communist Use of Jan Hus." *The Bohemian Reformation and Religious Practice* 6 (2007), pp. 283-296.

Odložilík, Otakar. "The Bethlehem Chapel in Prague: Remarks on its Foundation Charter." *Studien zur Älteren Geschichte Osteuropas* 2 (No.1, 1956), pp. 125-141.

Patapios, Hieromonk. "*Sub utraque specie*: The Arguments of John Hus and Jacoubek of Stříbro in Defense of Giving Communion to the Laity under both kinds." *Journal of Theological Studies*, n.s. 53 (No. 2, 2002), pp. 503-522.

Schaff, David S. *John Huss: His Life, Teachings and Death after Five Hundred Years.* New York: Scribner's, 1915.

Schofield, A.N.E.D. "The Case of Jan Hus." *The Irish Ecclesiastical Record* 109, 5th series (June, 1968), pp. 394-406.

Skodacek, Adolph August. *John Hus, Biblical Preacher.* Pittsburgh: Slovak Evangelical Union of America, 1952.

Šmahel, František and Ota Pavlíček, eds., *A Companion to Jan Hus.* Leiden: Brill, 2015.

Smolík, Josef. "Truth in History according to Hus' Conception." *Communio viatorum* 15 (1972), pp. 97-109.

Spinka, Matthew. *John Hus and the Czech Reform.* Chicago: University of Chicago Press, 1941.

_____. *John Hus' Concept of the Church.* Princeton: Princeton University Press, 1966.

_____. *John Hus: A Biography.* Princeton: Princeton University Press, 1968.

Workman, Herbert Brook. *The Dawn of the Reformation,* volume 2: *The Age of Hus.* London: Charles H. Kelly, 1902.

Wratislaw, A.H. *John Hus. The Commencement of Resistance to Papal Authority on the Part of the Inferior Clergy.* London: SPCK, 1882.

Zeman, Jarold K. *The Hussite Movement and the Reformation in Bohemia, Moravia and Slovakia (1350-1650): A Bibliographical Study Guide (With Particular Reference to Resources in North America).* Ann Arbor: University of Michigan Slavic Publications, 1977.

Index of Names

This is a small book and therefore does not merit a detailed comprehensive index. The listings below are restricted to the proper names of places and individuals mentioned in the narrative. The chief exception is Jan Hus, who is omitted, because he is referred to so frequently and often in general terms. The page numbers which appear in bold font refer to the visual images included in the book. Hus and the author are excepted.

About the Author

Thomas A. Fudge is the Professor of Medieval History at the University of New England in New South Wales, Australia. He has held prior academic appointments both in New Zealand and the United States, including a previous university professorial chair. He holds the PhD in history from Cambridge University and the PhD in theology from Otago University in New Zealand. He has written twelve monographs and contributed to more than 120 other publications. In 1992 he was co-founder of the biennial international symposium *The Bohemian Reformation and Religious Practice* (BRRP) which convenes in Prague during even numbered years. Recognized internationally as an authority on Jan Hus and Hussite history, he has written extensively on the Hussite period including: *The Magnificent Ride: The First Reformation in Hussite Bohemia* (Ashgate, 1998), *The Crusade Against Heretics in Bohemia* (Ashgate, 2002), *Jan Hus: Religious Reform and Social Revolution in Bohemia* (Tauris, 2010), *The Memory and Motivation of Jan Hus, Medieval Priest and Martyr* (Brepols, 2013), *The Trial of Jan Hus: Medieval Heresy and Criminal Procedure* (Oxford University Press, 2013), *Heresy and Hussites in Late Medieval Europe* (Ashgate, 2014), and the forthcoming *Jan Hus Between Time and Eternity: Reconsidering a Medieval Heretic* (Lexington Books, 2016).

During 2015, as part of the sexcentennial (600th) anniversary of the Jan Hus execution, he has been a Research Fellow at the Kulturwissenschaftlichen Kolleg (Institute of Advanced Studies) as well as the University of Constance in southern Germany.

He has presented lectures around the world in Australia, the United States, Germany, Switzerland, the Czech Republic, England, Canada, and with numerous invitations to places such as Switzerland, Argentina, and the Czech Embassy in Washington, DC. He was the keynote speaker for a lecture series in Germany in January. Fudge was also awarded a Research Fellowship for the second half of 2015 at Moravian College and Theological Seminary in Bethlehem, PA. He was the keynote speaker for the annual Moses Lectures in Bethlehem, the plenary speaker for two keynote lectures at the Jan Hus Symposium at Andrews University in Berrien Springs, Michigan, and one of three keynote speakers assigned to deliver the plenary lectures anchoring the Southeastern Medieval Association Conference convening in Little Rock, Arkansas (the others being Professor Peter S. Hawkins of Yale, and Professor Stephen Owen of Harvard). As part of the 2015 international Hus celebrations, he has also lectured at many other institutions in places as far afield as Oregon, Michigan, Pennsylvania, Texas, North Carolina, New Brunswick, England, Australia, and the Czech Republic.

His next book (in press) titled *Jerome of Prague and the Foundations of the Hussite Movement* will be published by Oxford University Press in 2016. Aschendorff Verlag in Münster, Germany intends to publish a German edition of this monograph.

About the Center for Christian Studies

The Center for Christian Studies (CCS) was established in 1970. Among its founders was Howard Macy (PhD, Harvard), now Emeritus Professor of Religion and Biblical Studies at George Fox University in Newberg, Oregon. CCS is a major adult education program of Reedwood Friends Church in Portland, Oregon. Its very well-established visiting and resident scholars programs have consistently featured multidisciplinary work with an important and intentional interface between the academy and the general public. The Center for Christian Studies operates on the firm belief that continuing education is a healthy, normative part of adult life. The Center's programs seek to stimulate adult learners both intellectually and spiritually through direct interaction with specialists who are trained and experienced in specific fields of study. Visiting scholars have included a number of well-known and influential thinkers from a variety of disciplines, which include historical, philosophical, theological, and biblical perspectives. Two of the prominent examples of scholars in residence at CCS are Karen Jo Torgeson and Diogenes Allen.

Karen Jo Torjeson is the Margo L. Goldsmith Professor of Women's Studies at Claremont Graduate University and former Assistant Professor of Patristic Theology at the University of Göttingen. She is a well-known authority in the broader field of early Christianity and holds the PhD (1982) from Claremont Graduate University. She is best known for her acclaimed monograph *When Women Were Priests: Women's Leadership in the Early Church and the Scandal of Their Subordination in the Rise of Christianity* (Harper/Collins, 1993).

Diogenes Allen (1932-2013) was a renowned scholar in the field of Philosophy of Religion. He was the Stuart Professor of Philosophy at Princeton Theological Seminary where he taught for 35 years. He held the PhD from Yale (1965) and was widely recognized as a leading international authority on the German philosopher Gottfried Leibniz. He was also regarded as an influential interpreter of thinkers such as Søren Kierkegaard and Simone Weil. Allen was widely published and was a prolific author with more than fifteen monographs to his credit along with numerous essays and shorter works.